Balance Amongst the Chaos

This book is dedicated to the person searching for inner peace who deserves a life of fulfillment. This book is dedicated to the person who strives to consistently provide for themselves and their loved ones. This book is dedicated to You.

# BALANCE AMONGST THE CHAOS

## Your Step-by-Step Guide to Wellbeing Through the Chakras

## Sarah Iaccarino

### Foreword by Greg Doyle

Balance Amongst the Chaos

Sarah Iaccarino

© Sarah Iaccarino 2021

www.healwithaligntherapies.com

aligntherapies.llc@gmail.com

Design and publishing support by www.AuthorSupportServices.com

Photos by Polina Levina

Cover illustration by Melanie Howarth

ISBN    978-1-922375-08-7 ppk   978-1-922375-09-4 hbk

 A catalogue record for this book is available from the National Library of Australia

# Foreword

For many of you, the notion of a chakra system permeating the physical human body, regulating its many systems and higher functioning, will be just that: a notion, an idea—perhaps even a strange picture you once saw in a strange book. What does it all mean, you may have asked yourself, eyes casting rolling dispersions in all directions. Well then, I put it to you: What if it were real, and what if it were to mean, essentially, everything....

We live in an energetic universe. Science attests to this. Everything is bouncing, meshing and interacting with one another. Even as human beings, we literally physically do this, day in, day out, constantly, incessantly, whether at home, at work, or at play. The game of energy is all pervading, around us and within us. This is what this book is all about. As a handbook to navigating life within a human body, finding *Balance Amongst the Chaos* is simply a rare, and utterly helpful, gem!

An energy healer myself of many years, I first met Sarah a few years ago, and was instantly struck by her ability to cut through to the core of an issue. This attribute shines through her writing. Sarah links the dots in such a way that it offers you, the reader, a practical, formulated and intensely doable approach to identifying, healing and managing your energies/ well-being through the landscape of the chakra system. This book explains these gateways of energy with a lucidity and actionable clarity that is indeed rare in the genre.

Resonance is a law of our cosmos. Put a room full of metronomes together, and they'll soon start ticking at exactly the same time. So it is with our systems. Feel good, and outer circumstances will begin to match your frequency, your vibration. Identifying the changes needed and putting them into place is key to shifting to a life of greater health, manifestation and abundance. This book is that key, opening the door to a world of possibilities well within your grasp. Enjoy!

**Greg Doyle is an Astral Traveler, Author of *Awakening the Giant Within - A Personal Adventure into the Astral Realms*, and a Reiki Master.**

# CONTENTS

## PART 3: THE STRATEGIES

## PART 4: APPLICATION

# Editor's Note

This book wasn't written to be read once. As a labour of love, it was inadvertently penned to become a lifelong companion — constantly re-read, dog-eared and referenced over different stages of your life. *Balance Amongst the Chaos* successfully endeavors to provide readers with a simple yet comprehensive guide to improving their physical and <u>mental</u> well-being.

The breadth this book covers means different sections will be relevant to the many phases you will go through in your lifetime. It's the reason why you can expect yourself to form a deep connection with your copy, likely to become a book 'with character'. Only you will know the stories behind the various rips, tears and stains.

The simplicity of this book should not be underestimated. It accommodates time-constrained people caught up in the whirlwind of modern life. Explaining complex ideas clearly and concisely is a very difficult thing to do — *Balance Amongst the Chaos* achieves this.

I suggest you read this book with an open mind and an adventurous approach. It's oozing with small changes you can make to improve your life. These lessons range from being generalized to dealing with very specific situations, and are easily implemented into your routine. For little effort, the professional and personal results are prodigious, allowing you to reach your full potential in all aspects and lead a rich and fulfilling life.

*Balance Amongst the Chaos* will stick with you for a lifetime and be there when you need it most.

**Angus Kennelly**

# PART 1

# BACKGROUND

**Understanding the relationship
between chakras and wellness**

# Introduction to Wellness

You are a very important person and highly regarded by your loved ones. You maintain copious professional and personal relationships, working vigorously to complete your commitments on a daily basis.

You strive to consistently deliver your best self, but life is chaotic. Due to the overstimulation from upholding multiple roles, your responsibilities can seem insurmountable. As a result, health and wellness may lack prioritization, falling last on your daily to-do list. Nevertheless, despite the disorder of life, you deserve optimal wellness.

The term wellness is commonly perceived to solely relate to one's physical health. Wellness typically evokes thoughts of weight management, blood pressure, diet, and exercise. Although these elements are vital for well-being, physical health is only one of eight components in the multidimensional sphere of wellness.

The eight-dimensional model of wellness was developed by the University of Michigan's Health Department in 2012, expanding from the original six-model established by Dr. Bill Hettler in 1976. The modern model of wellness consists of the physical, intellectual, spiritual, emotional, social, environmental, financial, and occupational elements of an individual's lifestyle. This model helps us build a personal foundation for establishing strong self-esteem and a sense of purpose. The overall quality of one's life is contingent on the development and amalgamation of all eight dimensions on a daily basis.

Throughout the chaos of life, it is understandable certain dimensions often take precedence over others. Nevertheless, negating a dimension for a prolonged period of time results in external and internal disharmony. A balanced integration of all dimensions of wellness supports an overall well-constructed quality of life.

# The Role of Chakras in Wellness

There is a method for simultaneously improving all eight dimensions of wellness, which is executed through activation of the chakra system. The chakras, invisible to the eye, are centers energy that keep the body, mind, and spirit in balance.

The chakras directly impact your overall well-being and require specific care for proper functionality. Activating the chakra system is a lengthy process incorporating specific practices into your daily routine. The activation occurs through the instillment of mindfulness techniques over a prolonged period of time, bringing forth self-awareness through the removal of energetic blocks in the body.

This awareness connects the body, mind, and spirit — creating unity within oneself — this is how inner peace is achieved.

Inner peace is a highly desired experience for human beings — easily attainable through chakra activation. Once inner peace is achieved, your body and mind begin to constantly crave this equilibrium, as it creates harmony in all areas of your life. This harmonious inner peace becomes an addictive feeling, as beneficial changes occur as an after-effect. These positive outcomes are continually accessible to those who mindfully practice various chakra cleansing habits.

Chakra activation derives from the implementation of proper nutrition, physical exercise, and meditation techniques. In regard to the chakra system, there are specific elements of nutrition, exercise, and meditation that efficiently cleanse the energy channels. The contents of this book teach the history of the seven main chakras, as well as surprisingly effective and practical methods to ignite the activation process. The lifestyle habits shared are straightforward and simple enough to incorporate into your busiest days.

The activation process is achievable for all and requires time, effort, and intention. Practice your meditations every morning, try a new recipe each week, challenge your body to different yoga postures and implement several healthy chakra healing habits. Your chakras will begin to activate, surfacing feelings of inner peace and alignment. Your physical and non-physical body will positively adapt to the minor lifestyle habits — the shift will be inevitable.

Allow this esoteric harmony to improve all capacities of your life, and you will begin to feel balance amongst all of life's chaos.

# The Law of Vibration

Before exploring the history and purpose of the chakras, it is imperative to understand the basic concepts of vibrational energy, or subtle energies.

This theory is thoroughly explained through the Law of Vibration, the second Law of the Universe. It states anything that exists in the universe, seen and unseen, is composed of pure energy and moves or vibrates in a pattern on various wavelengths. Everything — all matter, thoughts, feelings, emotions, and food — has its own specific vibrational frequency. The strength of the frequency depends on the surrounding energy.

This law explains that energy will attract similar energy (on the same vibrational frequencies). Lower vibrational energy attracts other low vibrations, and high vibrational energy attracts higher vibrations.

The human body consists of millions of molecules vibrating on a certain frequency. The frequency level the body vibrates on is directly contingent to the physical and mental health of that body. When the body and mind are properly cared for, they will vibrate on a high frequency and be free from illness. Mental and physical illnesses vibrate on an exceptionally low frequency. Subsequently, the vibrations of the body will decrease when experiencing physical or emotional stress.

All energy needs external energy to properly function. Similar to all matter, each chakra is a cluster of energy vibrating at a certain frequency. The level each chakra vibrates at is dependent on the energy the physical and emotional body receives.

The chakras will vibrate on a higher frequency, directly impacting the physical and emotional well-being of the individual, when they receive higher vibrational energies. These higher vibrational energies derive from nutritionally dense food, positive thinking, physical exercise, conscious action, and meditation.

Continue reading to explore the history of the chakra system, how the chakras influence your mental and physical well-being, and daily habits you can adopt to energize them.

# The Chakra System

The chakra system originates from India, starting in the year 1000 BC. Evidence of the power of the chakras was shared through the Vedas — more specifically Shandilya Upanishad and Cudamini Upanishad. These are ancient Sanskrit texts of the spiritual teachings and practices of Hinduism.

Knowledge of the chakra system evolved through oral tradition, becoming commonly recognized 2000 years ago with the emergence of the Tantra tradition. Prior to Tantra, the physical body was believed to be an obstacle obstructing spiritual evolution. Tantra embraces the physical body, regarding it as a vessel for enlightenment. It maintains the principle that spiritual transformation occurs through activation of the chakras, cleansing the physical body of impurities and guides the etheric body, or energetic body, to complete enlightenment.

Chakras are small triangles throughout the body formed by the intersection of energy channels. These channels are referred to as "nadis" in Indian tradition or "meridians" in Chinese tradition and run through the entire human body. The channels transfer vital energy, known as "prana", through the passageways, and are responsible for carrying energy to all sections of the body. The convergences of the nadis are believed to form around 80,000 chakras.

The seven major energy centers composing the main chakra system are critical because they contain innumerable intersections of the nadis. These intersections form circular shapes, similar to a wheel. This visual helps explain the translation of the Sanskrit text "chakra", meaning "spinning wheel".

These larger energy centers connect small chakras and nadis into a sphere-like shape that "spins" or rotates prana throughout the energetic body. The seven main chakras align the physical body along the length of the spine, beginning with the base and ending above the skull. Each main chakra is associated with a major organ and gland as well as a component of spiritual wellbeing to connect the physical and non-physical body.

Chakras act as gateways between the energy and the channel it travels through. They can be thought of as areas in the body that receive, retain, and distribute energy. As a result of the chaotic world we reside in, these areas can become blocked and imbalanced due to external situations, negative habits, and internal limitations.

When chakras are free of blockages, they are open, allowing prana to freely pass through the nadis.  However, if there is a blockage in a chakra, this stagnant energy triggers physical, mental, or emotional imbalances. These imbalances manifest in a wide variety of physical or psychological symptoms. The goal of chakra cleansing is to remove blockages by recognizing, managing, and eliminating these symptoms to improve overall quality of life.

## The importance of understanding your chakras

Chakra development, or activation, is a natural part of the evolution of a human being. The chakra system is a gateway for personal exploration and spiritual development. Understanding and properly caring for the chakras helps individuals utilize the power of the human body, strengthening the connection between the mind and physical body.

The chakras provide information that enlightens individuals about where emotional, physical, or spiritual blockages exist in their body. The location of these blockages indicate which components of wellness may be lacking in their lives. Learning where blockages exist and which dimensions of wellness are not receiving adequate attention helps to improve their current lifestyle and brightening those surrounding them — leading to positive evolution.

Evolution is an inevitable component of human nature. It is an innate desire for humans to develop both physically and spiritually throughout their time on earth. Adapting, learning, correcting mistakes, and expanding our mental capacities are important factors in reaching an enlightened state. Evolving spiritually creates a stimulating and compelling life for oneself as well as the awareness of how to attract a financially and emotionally abundant lifestyle.

Through spiritually evolving, you will become the director of your own fate and a leader for others. Growing and expanding past your physical and psychological barriers grants people surrounding you the opportunity to also improve themselves. This influential cycle perpetuates the evolution of humanity.

In regard to personal development, it is extremely important to understand all components of your physical and energetic body. You cannot evolve if there is blocked energy in your chakras. It is pivotal to heal from traumatic experiences, offer forgiveness to those who have wronged you, and absorb the life lessons that are presented to you. These actions help your body to release anger, grief, and fear, allowing it to begin healing.

When this process is ignited, your body loosens and your chakras begin to filter through stagnant energy that has created physical or psychological burdens. Your mind and spirit will be unable to evolve if your physical body is not healed. To spiritually evolve and attract abundance into your life, it is crucial to heal the specific part of your body, or chakra, retaining trauma.

## Common symptoms of blocked chakras

In order to sustain optimal health, the chakras must remain open and free of blockages so prana can easily transfer through the nadis. However, chakras often become blocked with stagnant energy and do not function as efficiently as they should. Stagnant energy builds up as a result of excess stress, substandard nutritional choices, past trauma, emotional distress, and a lack of physical exercise.

Your physical body remembers every single feeling it has ever experienced. Despite mentally or emotionally coping with pain, your physical body retains any trauma experienced. Regardless of the severity of the pain — whether it is from a disingenuous fight with your partner, a car accident, or sexual trauma — your physical body retracts, becoming tight and rigid as a defense mechanism to protect itself against harm. This physical denseness represents a blocked chakra and hinders the ability to spiritually evolve.

Blocked chakras create an imbalance in our lives. These imbalances appear as physical and psychological symptoms resulting from a diagnosed illness, traumatic life experience, emotional burden, physical injury, or societal conditioning.

Symptoms of blocked chakras range from self-doubt and anger, irritable bowel syndrome and asthma, to depression and post-traumatic stress disorder. When these symptoms are neglected for a prolonged period of time, they start to hinder your mental health and quality of life. Consequently, this hindrance begins to negatively impact external areas of your life — including romantic relationships, professional endeavors, financial responsibilities, and your social life.

# Understanding Energetic Blocks

An energetic block is a physical or emotional ailment one can experience. Ultimately, energetic blocks symbolize areas in your life involving stress, unhappiness, or resentment — meaning that area would likely benefit from improvement.

It does not take strenuous effort to distinguish where an energetic block exists in your body. It simply requires the willingness to candidly evaluate your life. Your energetic blocks can be reported by your spiritual healer, observed using the pendulum method (discussed in the following chapter), or distinguished through honest self-evaluation of your current lifestyle.

Distinguishing which chakras sustain blocked energy begins with observing the areas of your life that appear to be imbalanced. This requires genuine reflection on the dimensions of wellness which could be lacking attention.

Ask yourself the question, "Where could I improve myself and my life?" Let the answers guide you in creating awareness of your current needs. Review these questions and the one to first strike a nerve is where your attention should be directed.

## Questions for self-evaluation

Here are some self-evaluating questions:

- ❖ Does my job fulfill me?
- ❖ Am I challenged in my work?
- ❖ Am I living out my purpose?
- ❖ Am I happy in this relationship?
- ❖ Am I struggling to end a relationship or friendship?
- ❖ Am I generous or do I fear scarcity?
- ❖ Do I give with the expectation to receive something?
- ❖ Is my happiness contingent on the actions of my loved ones?
- ❖ Am I lonely?
- ❖ Do I seek attention from others to feel confident?
- ❖ Am I comfortable doing things by myself?
- ❖ Am I valuing materialism over stoicism?
- ❖ Do I use alcohol and drugs as escapism?
- ❖ Do I enjoy my social life or does it deplete me?
- ❖ Do I have any resentment or anger towards anyone or myself?
- ❖ Do I find myself often feeling impatient or short tempered?
- ❖ Am I comfortable in my body?
- ❖ Am I over exercising?
- ❖ Am I nourishing my body properly?
- ❖ Am I confident when I speak?
- ❖ Do I manage my stress efficiently?
- ❖ Am I sleeping well?
- ❖ Do I live in the present moment?
- ❖ Am I kind to myself?

Mark the questions that make you ponder your current lifestyle. The answers to these questions help draw awareness to your strengths and weaknesses as well as any physical or emotional symptom you are currently experiencing. All symptoms are connected to a specific chakra. The goal is to acknowledge any challenges you are currently facing and overcome that challenge by healing the chakra associated with your current symptoms.

In the following chapters, there is a list of common symptoms and typical behaviors associated with each chakra. First, honestly assess your lifestyle, present challenges, and active goals. Then, read the behaviors and challenges of each chakra and acknowledge if any currently resonate with you. This serves as a guide for which chakra needs healing.

From there, implement the tools provided to care for this chakra. Purchase the ingredients for the smoothie, practice the yoga asanas, try several of the healthy habits designated for that specific chakra, and write the affirmations down twice a day. Allow your physical and nonphysical body to acknowledge the effort you are exerting to address this area of your life.

Your chakras work for you. They simply need attention and devotion to healing.

## Energetic traffic jams

Activating the chakra system and moving blocked energy is not as complicated as it may appear. It is truly quite achievable once the process is understood and the proper tools are accumulated.

To better comprehend the esoteric flow that occurs within, take a moment to think outside of the body.

Visualize a moderately busy four-way intersection with traffic lights. There are multiple cars casually traveling on the road and all come to a stop as the traffic lights turn red. The cars are patiently waiting at the intersection to continue moving in their intended direction.

As a vehicle drives along a street and approaches a red light, it is required to stop.

Once the light turns green, vehicles may only continue traveling through the intersection if their fuel tanks are sufficiently filled. A vehicle will remain motionless at the intersection and unable to pass through if it does not have the minimum level of gasoline. If all the vehicles are low on gasoline they must park at the intersection. They cannot move until their fuel tank is adequately filled.

This will cause a traffic jam.

A traffic jam represents an energy block.

In order to avoid a traffic jam and allow all vehicles to continue traveling through the intersection, each car's fuel tank needs to be filled completely. The goal is to ensure all cars can continue traveling without any forced stops.

Now, relate this example back to the body. These intersections and traffic jams occur throughout the entire human body.

The streets that the cars travel on are the nadis.

The open space of the intersection, where the streets meet, is a chakra.

The vehicle, which travels on the road, represents prana.

The fuel that allows the vehicle to operate is composed of meditation, proper nutrition, and exercise.

The flow of energy in our non-physical body is similar to the flow of traffic during rush hour. When prana is flowing through the nadis and approaches a chakra, it is forced to stop. It will continue flowing through the chakra if there is no blockage. There will be no blockage present if all prana is provided an adequate amount of exercise, nutrition, and meditation.

The goal is to keep all prana flowing through the nadis and chakras without any forced stops.

It is your responsibility to ensure your energetic fuel tank is properly filled with exercise, nutrition, and meditation so your non-physical body can avoid energetic blocks (or metaphorically, "traffic jams").

# How to Read Your Chakras

There are two methods for efficiently reading your chakras and distinguishing which are energetically blocked. Foremost, it is always recommended to meet with a professional after authentically evaluating your current challenges and active goals.

Working with an experienced spiritual healer, reiki master, or craniosacral therapist every few months will distinguish where energetic blocks exist in the physical body. Bring your challenges and goals to these healers as their expertise will help further advancement in your healing journey. Routinely meeting with your healer and assessing all progress and any roadblocks is exceptionally advantageous for your emotional and spiritual wellness. These sessions will explain which chakras require further care, move stagnant energy from the body, and pass on holistic practices to serve your current needs.

Nonetheless, between healing sessions, chakra readings can also be done in the comfort of your own home. The only tool necessary is a **crystal pendulum**. Pendulums are crafted from different crystals or stones and are sold in various shapes and sizes. They have blunt edges and are attached to a leather or metal chain that can swing it in a circular motion. These can be purchased from a local crystal shop or spiritual store and are typically priced between fifteen and thirty dollars.

The energy in the crystal pendulum vibrationally responds to the energy in the chakras. The flow of energy in each chakra is distinguished by how wide the pendulum spins. When the pendulum is held above a chakra and fails to circulate, or only moves slightly, it signifies an energetic block. Conversely, when the pendulum circulates widely it shows a strong flow of energy. The direction that the pendulum spins is not significant for this practice, only how wide it spins.

Purchase a pendulum that attracts your eye and vibrates when you hold it. The temperature of your palm will warm and your fingers may tingle when you find the perfect pendulum. Keep it nearby and use it regularly to ensure it stays connected to the flow of your energy.

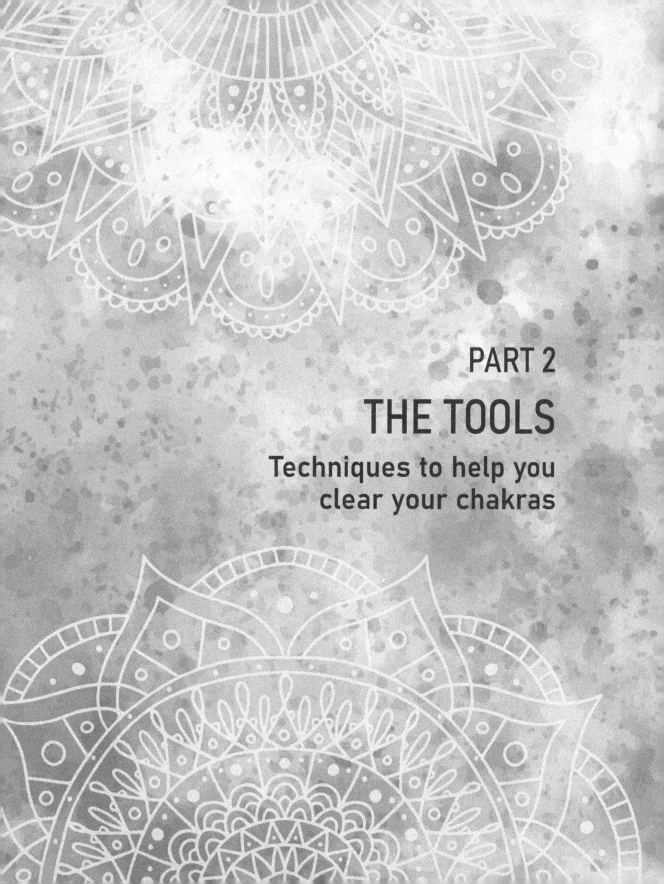

# PART 2

# THE TOOLS

**Techniques to help you
clear your chakras**

# The Tools

To energize your chakras, your energetic fuel tank needs to be filled with a variety of mindfulness practices. These include crystal therapy, the psychology of color, aromatherapy, nutrition, yoga and meditation.

When several healthy habits from each mindfulness practice are integrated into your daily lifestyle, your overall state of well-being will positively increase over time.

Here is an overview of each significant chakra-activating mindfulness practice.

# Crystal Healing

Crystal healing is a holistic therapeutic modality utilizing gemstones and crystals as conductors for positive energy flow throughout the body. Crystals and gemstones are solid molecular structures containing ions in a repetitive arrangement. These healing tools have crystalline lattices built within their atomic structure making them a consistent conductor of energy.

The body is energy, the chakras are energy, and crystals are energy. Everything is energy vibrating at different frequencies. Energy requires external sources of energy to function efficiently. The vibrational frequencies of the ions in crystals are exceptionally beneficial for the metaphysical energy of the human body. When the body is exposed to the high frequencies of crystals and gemstones, it produces a powerful flow of energy that can positively influence emotional health.

The healing energy of crystals will improve your wellbeing after consistent utilization. The benefits of crystal healing range from the stabilization of emotions to spiritual protection. It is important to always keep your crystals in close proximity so your body and mind can continuously absorb their healing powers. Over time their energy can help relieve anxiety, improve sleep cycles, release grief, and strengthen mental clarity through balancing your etheric energies.

There are countless methods for bringing the healing power of crystal energy into your daily life. It may be unrealistic to partake in an hour-long crystal meditation every day, but having your crystals in close proximity creates subtle positive changes for your wellbeing. The most convenient way to utilize their energetic powers is to keep them close by.

Here are several ways to incorporate crystal energy into your everyday life:

- ❀ Store several crystals underneath your pillows or on your bedside table to promote improved sleep cycles.
- ❀ Keep several on your work desk and reach for them when you need a mental break.
- ❀ Leave a few in your wallet/purse, backpack, or cup holder in your car. Hold them when you need extra support completing your responsibilities for the day.
- ❀ Decorate your bathroom with your favorite crystals so you see them at the beginning and end of your day.
- ❀ Always grab a few of your favorites to hold in your palms before starting your daily meditation practice.

## How to properly maintain your crystals

It is critical to respect and care for your crystal collection so they continue working efficiently. The more often a stone is used, the more energy is collected and stored in it. It is important to cleanse and recharge them often so they are always conducting positive energy. Ideally, crystals and stones should be cleansed once a month, but there is no hard and fast rule. Use your own judgement. We all have a unique relationship with our crystal collection, so our gut instincts are often right.

There are three simple methods for recharging your crystals:

1. Saltwater rinse - Salt has been utilized throughout history to banish unwanted or negativity energy, making it very effective for cleansing and recharging crystals. Fill a white or clear bowl with tepid water and mix in one tablespoon of rock, table, or sea salt. Gently place the stones in the saltwater, ensuring each one is submerged. Let them soak for 24 hours, remove and rinse with cold water, then pat dry.

2. Natural Light - Stones can be placed outside to absorb the natural light from the moon and sun at any time, but it is exceptionally powerful

when aligned with the full moon cycles. Place your stones outside in a safe area before nightfall and bring them inside before 10am. Direct sunlight may weaken the stone's surface so it is best to return them in the morning. Gently wash off any debris and pat dry.

3. Brown Rice - Fill a bowl with uncooked brown rice and bury the stones beneath the grains. Rice is believed to remove negative energy. Let them sit for 24 hours, then gently rinse and pat dry (make sure to discard the rice).

Ask about the cleansing methods for each stone upon purchase. The store clerk at your local crystal shop will be able to offer further insight and elaborate on the instructions listed for each crystal. All stones and crystals have specific steps for proper maintenance, and following the instructions ensures longevity and protection of your energetic tools.

# Chromotherapy

Colors have a prominent influence on human behavior and emotions. The reactions colors ignite in humans are directly related to psychological effects and cultural conditioning. However, certain colors draw different psychological and emotional responses, directly influencing your current moods.

Warm colors consist of red, orange, and yellow and typically stimulate feelings of passion, creativity, and enthusiasm. Cool colors are more subdued than warm colors, consisting of shades of green, blue, and purple. These colors often generate calming, relaxing, and peaceful feelings.

Understanding how certain colors directly impact our emotional health is pivotal in chakra activation. Utilize the significance of color psychology as another tool for emotional management and energizing blocked chakras.

## Color associations

Here is a breakdown of the emotions associated with the colors.

### Red

The color **red** is typically linked with danger, passion, anger and violence. It can ignite blood pressure and enhance human metabolism. Red is a strong color and often symbolizes importance and urgency.

### Orange

**Orange** is a secondary color strongly affiliated with creativity. It is more gentle and friendly than red, often signifying change because it is deeply connected to changing seasons like autumn. Due to its connection to the fruit, orange is also associated with vitality and health.

### Yellow

**Yellow** is a warm color connected to feelings of hope, happiness, and triumph. It is a gentle primary color, igniting feelings of peace and serenity.

## Green

Green is an earthing/grounding color combining the calmness of blue hues and the electrifying energy of yellow. Green can represent abundance, renewal, and growth as well as contrary feelings of envy or jealousy. Brighter shades of green are vitalizing and energizing, while olive or hunter greens inspire more calming and earthing/grounding emotions.

## Blue

The emotions associated with the color blue are contingent on the shade. Light blue evokes feelings of serenity, trust, and authority. It connects a person to their intuitions whilst strengthening empathy, confidence, and communication.

The color indigo is a combination of dark blue and violet. It is an exceptionally spiritual color, encouraging deep intuitive thoughts, wisdom, and self-mastery. It stimulates creative thinking and is connected to organization, rituals, and increased perception.

## Violet

**Violet** is linked to transformation, divinity, and imagination. It's the primal color of spirituality, igniting feelings of mysticism, wisdom, security, and contentment.

Understanding and implementing the concepts of color psychology is advantageous in emotional management. Utilize this information accordingly and choose colors complimenting your current ambitions and intentions.

# Using colors in your life

Pay attention to the role colors play in your life. Notice the color scheme in your living room, bathroom, and bedrooms.  Acknowledge how you feel in each room. Start to become aware of the way different colors make you feel. Decorate your home and dress with intention.

Implementing these minor changes can make significant improvements over time:

- ❀ Switch out your black, white, or gray coffee mug for a vibrant yellow, blue, or lavender one. Your subconscious mind will enjoy this subtle change when you drink your morning coffee or evening tea.
- ❀ Add relaxing colors to your bedroom and living room space. Try adding some colorful pillows, blankets or lamps, or consider painting the walls a mood lifting color.
- ❀ Decorate the home with plants and flowers. The greenery supports the heart chakra, creating a calming ambiance. Explore the local thrift shop and buy a few colorful pots to grow your new plants in.
- ❀ Purchase a colorful yoga mat for your daily stretches. Pick one that attracts your eye, so you enjoy stepping on it every day.
- ❀ Paint your fingernails and toenails any color that complements your current moods. Keep it exciting.
- ❀ Enhance your outfit with colorful accessories to amplify your moods.

# Aromatherapy

Aromatherapy is a holistic healing treatment utilizing aromatic plant extracts to enhance physical, mental, and emotional health.

The term was founded by Rene-Maurice Gattefosse, a French perfumer and chemist, in the early 1920s. He developed methods using essential oils to accelerate the healing process after severely burning his hand. However, the utilization of plant extracts dates to ancient Egyptians, who were very knowledgeable about the beneficial healing properties of botanics. Throughout the past few centuries, biochemists have carried out scientific research on various components of plants and their ability to positively impact psychological and physical well-being.

Due to the advancement of aromatherapy over the past several decades, there is vast research connecting specific essential oils to various emotional or physical ailments. The utilization of essential oils cannot replace the importance of pharmaceutical or medical intervention. However, they play a significant role as effective tools in the healing process, due to their mood boosting abilities.

Similar to the effects candles and incense have on the atmosphere of a room, essential oils positively uplift your mental space. A brief inhale, applying them to your skin with a carrier oil, or purifying the air with an essential oil diffuser are subtle-yet-beneficial methods for improving breathwork, alleviating anxiety, and decreasing your heart rate. When routinely incorporated into your lifestyle, essential oils can help decrease depression, increase libido, lower blood pressure, reduce inflammation, and improve digestion after a prolonged period of time.

Essential oils are one of the most convenient mindfulness tools because they're accessible and simple to use. Initially, investing in high quality essential oils may appear fruitless and overpriced — costing close to thirty dollars for a three-ounce jar. Nevertheless, a small amount of oil can last for nine to twelve months, depending on how frequently it is used. As well as being a cost-effective investment, essential oils are ideal for traveling, as they do not occupy any more space than a tube of Chapstick and can be used at any time.

Purchasing and utilizing oils for mental and physical health purposes is truly a cost-efficient investment based on their convenience and effectiveness.

## Using essential oils

There are numerous ways you can easily incorporate essential oils into your daily lifestyle:

- Add a few drops of oil to your hand moisturizer and use after washing your hands.
- Experiment with body lotion by adding a combination of your favorite oils to a carrier oil or body lotion.
  - Carrier oils are extracted from plants and used to dilute essential oils, as some are too potent to use directly on your skin. Most carrier oils are unscented or lightly scented and do not interfere with the properties of the essential oils. Coconut oil, sweet almond oil, apricot kernel oil, sunflower oil, and olive oil are examples of carrier oils that are beneficial in deeply moisturizing your skin. Typically, 15 to 20 drops of the essential oil in a carrier oil or unscented body lotion will suffice.
- Create a calming spray by diluting water with 10 drops of your favorite oil in a small spray bottle and always keep it nearby.
  - Spray your pillows before falling asleep, your car before going to work, or the aura around your head prior to a stressful meeting.
- Add peppermint or eucalyptus oil to any homemade hygiene or household product such as toothpaste, mouthwash, deodorant, laundry detergent, or hand soap for additional calming remedies.

There are countless ways essential oils can be embedded into your mindfulness habits. Get creative, but be cautious. Before incorporating an essential oil or carrier oil into your daily routine, conduct a patch test to examine if your body will have any reaction to that particular oil. Simply add a few drops of the oil on your wrist or behind your ear and cover it with a bandage.

Examine the patch 24 hours later to check if a rash or irritation has developed. If so, cleanse the area thoroughly and avoid using this oil in your regimen. Additionally, avoid using any essential oils directly on the eyelids or lips and use reasonable judgement when ingesting the oils. Some practitioners suggest a few drops of essential oils in your coffee, tea, or water have beneficial effects, but others do not recommend this practice. Consult an experienced aromatherapist with any questions or concerns before incorporating a new oil into your mindfulness routine.

# Nutrition

Food is a vital tool for energizing and healing the chakras. The chakras require external energy for proper functionality, and they directly respond to the vibrational energy food possesses. When the chakras are nourished with healthy, living food they will efficiently transfer prana throughout the body.

It is exceptionally important to be consciously aware of the food you fuel your body with. The food you ingest can either positively influence your physical, emotional, and spiritual body or slowly damage it.

There are several ways to seek advice on improving your nutritional habits. The most beneficial outlet would be to work closely with a registered dietician or nutritionist. These professionals are experts on the chemical breakdown of food, and can personally create a meal plan to suit your current physical and mental needs. Nevertheless, there are countless healthy eating habits you can incorporate into your daily routine if this resource is unavailable for you.

## Using food for wellbeing

Keep these ideas in the forefront of your mind while grocery shopping and preparing meals:

- Food is energy.
  - Every item of food exists on its own vibrational frequency and directly impacts the frequency of the chakras.
  - Fruits and vegetables exist at a higher frequency than processed foods because they are living foods that are grown from earth with the energy from the sun. Contrarily, processed food is manufactured from a variety of chemicals and substances and vibrates on a lower frequency than fresh food.
  - Do not expect your physical and emotional body to perform efficiently if they are fueled with genetically modified foods high in sugars and sodium. The vibrational frequency of your body is directly influenced by the energy it is given.
- Fuel yourself based on your current lifestyle.
  - Are you currently working long hours, expecting a baby, or training for a fitness event? Your body and mind might need additional food to counteract the stress it is enduring. Eat accordingly.
  - Do you perform to your best ability if you undereat or overeat? The amount of food consumed is crucial in energizing your physical and emotional body. Pay attention to your energy levels after finishing a meal. Feeling lethargic, experiencing more hunger, or

craving sweets are signs of a nutritional imbalance and should be evaluated.

❀ Food directly impacts your emotional health.

❁ Evaluate how you are feeling physically, emotionally, and spiritually before entering the grocery store.

❁ Avoid purchasing any items of food that serve as escapism for your current feelings.

❁ Make a conscious decision to fill your grocery cart with foods that will strengthen your mental health.

❁ The food you consume impacts your outward appearance and influences your confidence, performance, and identity. Living food - such as fruits, vegetables, nuts, and grains - boosts energy and lifts your mood, whilst processed and genetically modified foods contribute to lethargy and brain fog.

❁ Remember that your gut microbiome is as unique as your fingerprints. There is not one meal plan that fits everyone perfectly. It is important to experiment with different foods and dietary habits. Observe how your body and mind respond to various foods and eat what makes you feel good.

❀ Treat your body like a gift.

❁ Food is healing and has a remarkable effect on the chakras.

❁ Your body is a vessel for enlightenment and spiritual evolution. It is an incredibly significant tool that permits the activation of the innate power that is achievable for all.

As you continue reading, you will find a list of healthy foods, smoothie recipes, and beneficial teas to nourish each chakra.  Use this information to guide you through your chakra activation, meal prepping, and weekly grocery shops. Aim to add a few healthy nutritional habits into your daily routine, then gradually incorporate more over time.

# Yoga

Yoga is a combination of physical, mental, and spiritual disciplines originating in ancient India. The desired outcome of this mindfulness practice is to deepen the communication between the individual and their higher self, also referred to as Source, Spirit, or God. This occurs through the connection of physical movement to structured breathwork helping the mind disconnect from the body.

The practice of yoga is exceptionally advantageous in activating the chakra system. The physical asanas filter blocked energy in the lower chakras while simultaneously energizing the third eye and crown chakras through meditative, intentional breathwork.

The philosophy of yoga teaches that the "Ego", also referred to as the conscious mind, is responsible for logical thinking, analysis, and mental chatter (a prominent cause of internal suffering humans endure). The goal of a dedicated yoga practice is to challenge the physical body and deliver tranquility of the mind through overriding mental chatter created by the Ego.

Yoga strengthens the subconscious mind, storing intuition and long-term memory, whilst silencing conscious thought so one can achieve mental clarity deepening their relationship with their higher self.

The Sun Salutation or *Surya Namaskār* is the perfect place for new students to explore their practice. It is a sequence of asanas that simultaneously awakens the entire body. Being a traditional vinyasa flow, it can be utilized as a warm-up for a full yoga class or as a complete practice on its own.

It is often performed in the early hours of the morning to bring awareness to the physical and emotional body, but can be performed at any time. The most imperative element of the sun salutation is the student's breathwork. It is important to cycle through rounds of even and controlled rounds of inhalation and exhalation.

Alternate between each as your body transitions through the postures. The most popular variations of the sun salutation are *Surya Namaskār A* and *Surya Namaskār B.* The movements of these flows activate each chakra while bringing awareness to the entire body.

## Sun A Flow - Surya Namaskār A

1. Mountain pose [Tadasana]

2. Tall mountain pose [Urdvha Hastana] **Inhale**

3. Standing forward fold [Uttanasana] **Exhale**

4.   Half forward fold [Ardha uttanasana] **Inhale**

5.   Plank pose [Kumbhakasana] Exhale. Inhale as you transition down to the ground.

6.   Four limb staff pose [Chatturunga dandasana] **Exhale**

7.  Exhale as the entire body lowers to the ground transitioning into a backbend.

8.  Upward facing dog [Urdhva mukha shvanasana] **Inhale**

9.  Downward facing dog [Adho mukha shvanasana] **Exhale. 5 deep breaths**

10. Half forward fold [Ardha uttanasana] **Inhale**

11. Standing forward fold [Uttanasana] **Exhale**

12. Tall mountain pose [Urdvha Hastana] Inhale as the upper body rises to standing one vertebrae at a time.

13. Mountain pose [Tadasana] Exhale as the arms lower down to your sides.

# Sun B Flow - Surya Namaskār B:

1. Mountain pose [Tadasana] **Hold for 5 breaths**

2. Chair pose [Utkatasana] **Inhale**

3.   Standing forward fold [Uttanasana] **Exhale**

4.   Half forward fold [Ardha uttanasana] **Inhale**

5.   Plank pose [Kumbhakasana] **Exhale**. Inhale as you transition down to the ground keeping the elbows tucked tight to your sides.

6. Four limb staff pose [Chatturunga dandasana] Embrace the core and activate the legs as you slowly lower to the ground.

7. Exhale as the entire body transitions to the ground preparing for your backbend.

8. Upward facing dog [Urdhva mukha shvanasana] **Inhale**

9.  Downward facing dog [Adho mukha shvanasana] **Exhale**

10. Warrior I right leg [Virabhadrasana I] Inhale as the arms float down to frame the front leg transitioning into a high plank pose. In one fluid movement, lower halfway down to four limb staff pose.

11. Four limb staff pose [Chatturunga dandasana]

12. Exhale as the entire body lowers down to the ground transitioning into a backbend.

13. Upward facing dog [Urdhva mukha shvanasana] **Inhale**

14. Downward facing dog [Adho mukha shvanasana] **Exhale**

15. Warrior I left leg [Virabhadrasana I] Inhale as your arms flow down to frame the front foot moving into a high plank pose. In one fluid movement, lower halfway down to four limb staff pose embracing the core the entire time.

16. Four limb staff pose [Chatturunga dandasana]

17.  Exhale as the entire body transition to the ground preparing for a backbend.

18.  Upward facing dog [Urdhva mukha shvanasana] **Inhale**

19.  Downward facing dog [Adho mukha shvanasana] **Exhale. Hold for 5 breaths**

20. Half forward fold [Ardha uttanasana] **Inhale**

21. Standing forward fold [Uttanasana] **Exhale**

22. Chair pose [Utkatasana] **Inhale**

23. Mountain pose [Tadasana] **Exhale**

Complete this flow in full every time you step on your mat. Repeat the Sun B flow as many times as necessary to help stimulate the physical and emotional body, stabilize breath patterns, ease any anxiety, and connect back to yourself. Take your time and focus on building a strong breath pattern of equal inhalations and exhalations.

# The eight 'limbs' of yoga

Yoga is a complex practice that's about more than stretching the physical body and strengthening the core. It teaches numerous methods for living a fulfilled life, releasing stress from the body, and freeing the mind of attachments.

In Pantajali's '*Yoga Sutra*', there is an eight-fold path enlightening individuals on various moral and ethical guidelines for embodying the philosophy of yoga. Each limb depicts a different aspect of the practice that, when combined, all lead to freedom and enlightenment. These guidelines support yoga practitioners in leading a meaningful and abundant life.

Remember these elements as you start to incorporate yoga into your daily mindfulness routine:

1. Yamas - moral and ethical code of personal conduct

    ❁ Ahisma [non-violence] - no harmful words, actions or thoughts.
    ❁ Satya [truthfulness] - speak truthfully and not share criticism.
    ❁ Asteya [non-stealing] - physical things as well as time or relationships.
    ❁ Brahmacharya [moderation or chastity] - conscious in celibacy or monogamy.
    ❁ Aparigrapha [greedlessness] - do not hoard and avoid greediness.

2. Niyamas - attitudes towards ourselves and the development of self discipline

    ❁ Shaucha [cleanliness] - internal and external cleanliness.
    ❁ Santousha [contentment] - acceptance, compassion, and non-judgement.
    ❁ Tapas [self-discipline] - discipline in any practice that generates positive change.
    ❁ Swadhyaya [self-study] - constantly self evaluate and consciously improve yourself. Analyze your personality, assess your Ego and acknowledge past mistakes.
    ❁ Ishwara-pranidhana [devotion to God] - find devotion to yourself so you can silence the Ego, experience a relationship with God and devote your life to loving others.

3. Asanas - bodily postures

&#x2698; Any posture where you feel relaxed and alert at the same time. It is essential to be present in each asana and concentrate on the contracting muscles in each asana.

4. Pranayama - breath control

&#x2698; Breath energizes the chakras and vitalizes the body through the cardiopulmonary system. Controlling breath through lengthy inhalations and exhalations is beneficial in calming the nervous system, regulating emotions, and improving mental clarity. It is critical to concentrate on breathwork in every asana. With every exhale, deepen your posture by flexing your muscles and pushing your body a little further into the pose.

5. Pratyahara - conscious withdrawal of energy from the senses

&#x2698; This practice does not encourage you to avoid stimulation, but to acknowledge mentally stimulating situations and consciously choose your response to them. When practicing the asanas, pratyahara occurs once you close your eyes and focus internally on quieting the mental chatter and direct all attention to the asana — this takes time and practice. Through this practice, all five senses are quieted, sending a message to the body that it is safe to heal and recover from stress.

6. Dharana - concentration

&#x2698; After withdrawing our senses, our minds can completely concentrate on a single focal point, whether it is a vision, object, or idea. This helps the mind enter a deep state of tranquility, which filters distractions from the outside world — bringing you closer to yourself and God.

7. Dhyana - meditation on the Divine

&#x2698; This practice is a continuous, uninterrupted flow of consciousness towards a chosen object. This intense concentration helps you transcend into deep delta brain waves guiding the body and mind to enter an absolute meditative state.

8. Samadhi - union with the Divine

❀ A state of bliss is achieved when you become unified with your higher self and the conscious mind is no longer present. This is where one experiences complete peace within themselves and feels more connected with God than their physical body. One is not aware they are in this state of connection until the Ego returns and ascends the mind back into beta brain waves.

Write these limbs down and keep the list wherever you engage in your daily yoga practice. Make a habit of reviewing it before you start each session and plan how to bring the philosophy of yoga off the mat and into your everyday life. Through consistent practice, engaging in the physical movements and embodying the philosophy of yoga, you will significantly improve your wellbeing, and activate the chakra system.

As you begin your yoga journey it is beneficial to prioritize breathwork, concentration, and patience. Yoga students practice this philosophy to not only physically advance through the asanas, but to improve in all other areas of life. This mindfulness practice will strengthen the connection between body and mind by relieving physical pain whilst increasing muscular strength and mental clarity.

# Meditation

Meditation is an ancient practice that strengthens cognitive abilities through controlling the conscious mind. It builds awareness, mental clarity, tranquility, and self-actualization for individuals through the implementation of specific mindfulness techniques such as breathwork, visualizations and trataka or mantra repetition.

Regular meditation positively impacts mental health by reducing anxiety and depression while simultaneously strengthening the connection between body and mind. When performed correctly and routinely, meditation can move brain waves from a higher to a lower frequency — which can change the way you feel.

## How meditation affects the brain

During meditation, the brain does not process information as actively as normal because these mindfulness techniques alter the electrical activity of the brain. This is due to the fluctuations in the five brain waves, which change according to different activities and emotions. The five brain waves are alpha, beta, theta, gamma, and delta.

### Alpha waves

**Alpha waves** have a frequency range of 8 to 12 Hz and are the most common to occur at the beginning of meditation. These waves promote relaxation as they lower the production of stress hormones. When these waves activate, your heart rate and blood pressure reduce, allowing the nervous system to slow down.

### Beta waves

**Beta waves** actively dominate your brain when you're engaged in problem-solving, decision making and focused mental activity. They range from a frequency of 12 to 38 hertz and activate when your brain is fixed on cognitive tasks and external stimulation. These waves improve concentration and strengthen situational awareness; however, they also have the potential to produce feelings of stress, anxiety, and restlessness.

## Theta waves

**Theta waves** range from a frequency of 3 to 8 Hertz and are responsible for activating the third eye chakra. They keep you calm and focused by providing a tranquil mental state, strengthening intuition, and promoting creativity. Theta waves are activated when you engage in automatic tasks like washing hair, vacuuming, making the bed, or folding laundry. Your mind can experience a deep spiritual connection at Theta — it's an optimal state for visualizations and manifestations.

## Gamma waves

**Gamma brain waves** are responsible for deep concentration and high levels of cognitive functionality. These waves range from 25 to 100 Hertz, mostly residing around 40 Hz in humans. Every brain sustains gamma activity, but the amount of gamma waves produced varies on the individual. People with high gamma wave activity have a strong sense of control and are exceptionally intelligent. These waves have been linked to a strong memory and mental processing, efficient communication abilities, and positive emotions.

## Delta waves

The **Delta frequency**, which is the slowest brain wave vibration, ranges up to 3 Hertz. These waves increase the amount of melatonin and DHEA, two pivotal hormones our bodies naturally produce to heal itself. Delta waves occur during transcendental meditation and deep, dreamless slumber. These brain frequencies are the realm of the unconscious mind — a gateway to the universal and collective subconscious.

During meditation, the brain does not process information as actively as it normally does. As your rhythmic breathing alters, your mind receives more oxygen and your brain wave frequencies begin to fluctuate. Throughout meditation, your brain predominantly shows Theta waves. These waves promote a relaxed state of mind whilst strengthening intuitive abilities and the connection between body and mind.

As the brain begins to transform from the benefits of meditation, we begin to see positive impacts from incorporating this practice over a prolonged period of time. The benefits of regular meditation including producing more grey matter in the hippocampus and frontal areas of the brain. Grey matter is a nerve tissue serving as a generator of information in the brain. It is composed of neuronal cell bodies and unmyelinated axons, which carry signals and information between the cell bodies.

Grey matter encompasses areas in the brain involved with functionality of muscles, awareness of emotions, sensory perception, and memory. An increase of grey matter positively impacts an individual's wellbeing by increasing the regulation of emotions, improving focus, strengthening memory, increasing confidence and building a stronger sense of purpose.

## Developing a meditation practice

The key to developing a strong meditation practice is becoming comfortable with silence. Silence is exceptionally powerful and beneficial in building a successful meditation practice that helps individuals consolidate their relationship with themselves.

This is because extended moments of silence allow their conscious and subconscious mind to pause and relax. As the mind rests, decision making abilities, self-awareness and self-compassion grow. Silence helps an individual become more mindful which is essential to developing an effective meditation practice.

There are several important measures to take prior to implementing a meditation practice into your daily routine. First, begin by honestly evaluating your experience with meditation and comfortability with silence. If you are just embarking on your meditation practice, it is important to find a style that does not overwhelm or exasperate you.

As a beginner, try simpler styles, like trataka or breathwork, for a shorter period of time. It is best to master these techniques for five, ten, or fifteen-minute increments before exploring more complex styles.

Starting with longer or more challenging practices may be intimidating, leading to feelings of inadequacy. For example, if you attempt to engage in an hour-long silent session, as a beginner, you are likely to be unable to complete it and feel disappointed with yourself. It is important to start with a simpler practice that fits your current meditation experience. The success of this wellness activity is contingent on how well it matches your lifestyle. Starting a meditation practice that fails to resonate with you and your current routine can potentially lead to frustration, doubt, and defeat.

There are various methods of meditation scientifically proven to reduce stress while improving overall well-being. Explore these different meditation techniques favorable for beginners:

# Breathwork

Despite there being countless things in life outside of your control, you will always have control of your breathing patterns. Efficient breathing patterns help reduce stress, increase concentration, and improve vitality when practiced regularly.

As a beginner, it is paramount to learn to breathe through the nostril passageways. Practicing breathwork through nostril breathing is better for overall health compared to breathing through the mouth.

Nostril breathing allows the body to absorb more oxygen as it engages the lower lungs. When the lower lungs are activated, the cells receive more oxygen helping support proper tissue and organ function. Additionally, the engagement of the lower lungs promotes a calming effect on the body and mind because the parasympathetic nerve receptors exist there.

When these nerves are activated, the brain receives a message to release calming hormones to combat stress and anxiety. Contrarily, open mouth breathing stimulates sympathetic nerves activating cortisol, a detrimental stress hormone.

When the brain releases cortisol, the body believes it is in danger and does not inhale an adequate amount of oxygen. This reaction causes excess anxiety while increasing stress and inflammation.

## Nostril breathing

Practice this nostril breathing technique:

* Sit in a comfortable, upright position.
* Close the eyes halfway and release any tension from the eyebrows.
* Keeping the eyes closed halfway, focus your attention on the tip of your nose. With your lips closed, lower the shoulders from the ears, remove the tongue from the roof of the mouth and unclench the jaw.
* Taking 5 long counts to inhale — breathe in through the nostrils while simultaneously expanding the stomach.
* When you reach the fifth count, pause for one additional moment before exhaling through the nostrils for another five counts. This counts as one breath.
* Continue this pattern until you lose count of your breaths. As soon as your concentration breaks and you forget which number breath you are on, end your meditation practice for the day.
* Document the day, time, and how many breaths you counted.
* Challenge yourself to beat this number the following day.

Breath control requires consistent practice and patience, but has profound effects on your mental and physical health. Awareness and strengthening of your breathing patterns will positively help you in everything you do. When breathwork is incorporated into your daily mindfulness routine, you rely on your breath for regulating emotions, avoiding a reaction, and making decisions.

# Affirmations and intention setting

Setting an intention is the act of stating a goal you intend to accomplish through your actions and behaviors. An intention is something you desire to bring into your existence. It is a commitment you make with yourself.

An affirmation is an "I am" statement written in the present tense. It consists of positive words and affirms something already exists. An affirmation is an intention written as if it has already been accomplished.

## Examples:

**Intention**: I want to be nicer to myself.
**Affirmation**: I am beautiful. I am worthy. I love myself as I am.

**Intention**: I want people to genuinely hear me when I speak.
**Affirmation**: I am intelligent and there is value in my words. I am a strong communicator.

**Intention:** I just want to lose this extra weight and feel more confident in my body.
**Affirmation:** I am already living in my dream body. I am healthy.

**Intention:** I want to be in a healthy relationship with someone who admires and respects me.
**Affirmation:** I am in Love with my partner. I am happy in this relationship.

**Intention:** I would like more time to do the things I love.
**Affirmation:**  I am free.

**Intention:** It would be a dream to make a living from my hobbies. I want to work for myself.
**Affirmation:** My business is lucrative and successful. I am passionate about my career and am earning money doing what I love.

## Asking vs believing

Setting an intention is the act of goal planning and asking for positive change. Speaking an affirmation convinces yourself that you have already accomplished that goal or received what you have been asking for.

Affirmations help intentions manifest quicker through manipulation of the subconscious mind. The purpose of an affirmation is to subtly and consistently convince the mind and body it has already achieved the intended goal.

## Creating a new intention

❀  Take several moments to reflect on your current wheel of wellness. Write out all eight dimensions of wellness and list the positive and negatives of each. Choose a dimension to prioritize for the next several months and set an intention to strengthen it.

❀  Use these questions as a guide:

  ❀  What mindfulness activities would help improve this dimension of wellness?

  ❀  What needs to be removed from my life? What ritual should I add to my daily routine?

  ❀  What emotion am I not experiencing that I wish to?

  ❀  Do I need guidance on any upcoming decisions? What do I need clarity on?

❀  Set a daily or weekly intention based on your current emotions and responsibilities.

❀  Ask yourself these questions:

  ❀  What would I like to bring into my life today and this upcoming week?

  ❀  What happened today that I need help overcoming, releasing, or accepting?

  ❀  What is happening tomorrow that I need support with?

There is always an opportunity to grow and improve your life on a daily basis. Reflect on which area needs development and set an intention to enhance it. Write down your intention and then create an affirmation from it. Repeat the affirmation continuously. Memorize it. Write it down every morning upon waking and every evening before falling asleep. Embody the affirmation you have set. Believe it has already come to you.

## Trataka

Trataka is a tantric method of meditation stimulating the third eye and promoting various psychic abilities by generating energy in that chakra. A beginner version of trataka meditation is staring at a candle flame.

This can be performed in a quiet room or while relaxing in a bathtub. Ensure all technology is turned off and there are no artificial lights on. Light a candle and simply watch the flame. Continuously breathe in and out through the nasal passageways deepening your breath with every inhale.

Concentrate on the flame. Allow your breath and vision to support your mind in focusing on the flame. Notice the auras surrounding the flame and watch the colors transform. Engage in this practice until your mind loses attention. Close your eyes and rest, continuing to visualize the flame and focusing on your breathwork. Begin again or simply rest for the remainder of your meditation practice.

## Releasing resistance to meditation

Most people do not meditate. They attempt to "empty their brain" and simply cannot "clear their thoughts". This is not the purpose of meditation as it is not intended to "silence your thinking". Similar to how your heart naturally beats, your brain naturally produces thoughts — it is not designed to stop thinking.

The mind is restless and creates undesirable emotions of anxiety, depression, and fear if it is not actively monitored. The purpose of meditation is to **control** your thoughts, thus controlling the mind. Consciously monitoring and training your brain waves activates advantageous abilities through the subconscious mind.

Your subconscious mind is exceptionally powerful. It is a gateway for communication with your higher self and is a data-bank for every memory, experience, skill, and emotion ever experienced. Your subconscious is responsible for creating quality of life, storing perspective [optimistic or pessimistic outlook], system of beliefs, and self-image.

When it receives affirmations, compassion, and gratitude, it produces a positive mental space and attitude towards life. Contrastingly, the subconscious mind will create a pessimistic viewpoint and burdensome life if constantly absorbing negative, judgmental, fear-based, or angry thoughts. Your subconscious can be controlled through adopting empowering beliefs, practicing gratitude, stress-management, and regular meditation.

Incorporating a meditation practice into your routine does not need to be a daunting or complicated process. However, it does need to be integrated well if you wish to fully reap the benefits of meditation. Once you have researched and tried different methods — whether that be breathwork, chakra meditation, guided videos on YouTube, trataka, or repetitive affirmations — timing and location are critical to prolonged success.

You will encounter roadblocks if you attempt to incorporate these practices while your external and internal environments are cluttered. As a beginner meditator, it is important to create a personal, quiet, and safe space. Any situation compromising your attention and hindering full concentration on the practice should be avoided.

Politely requesting space from family members and friends is highly encouraged. This is your meditation space and your practice. It is okay to turn your phone on airplane mode for fifteen minutes or lock your bedroom door as you begin to explore the depths of your subconscious mind. Creating a meditation corner and prioritizing this practice whilst seeking respect from your peers for these new habits may even encourage them to consider starting meditation, themselves.

As your meditation skills strengthen, various thoughts and feelings will surface throughout your practice. This is normal and is the sole purpose of meditation. You are supposed to acknowledge these emotions. Through silence and stillness, messages come to you as a roadmap for where to focus your energy going forward.

Document the emotions, questions, or inspiration you received throughout the practice and include the date and time. This journal entry does not need to be extensive, but is beneficial in reflecting on various feelings, inspiration, breakthroughs, and overall progress of your meditation practice.

This journaling serves as a powerful tool for distinguishing the ideas you should pursue, past trauma requiring healing, or certain areas of life needing improvement from extra attention. Your subconscious mind is asking you to explore and address everything that arises. These feelings are important for chakra activation, serving as a guide for the areas of your life calling for work.

PART 3

# THE STRATEGIES

## How to work with each chakra in depth

# Introducing the Seven Main Chakras

As you begin to immerse yourself into the tools for cleansing and activating your chakras, it is pivotal to completely accept the physical and spiritual connection each has on your well-being.

Each chakra plays a separate, yet significant, role in each dimension of wellness, represents a spiritual life lesson, and depicts a common challenge for all human beings. A clear understanding of each role will advance the activation process, illuminate the challenges one must overcome on this life path, and strengthen the connection between body and spirit.

Just as everything is composed and influenced by energetic exchanges, the chakras move at different vibrational frequencies and directly influence the vibration of your physical and emotional body. The lower three chakras signify survival, creativity, action, and power. The middle chakra, the heart center, signifies compassion and is a gateway between the upper and lower chakras. The upper three chakras vibrate at higher frequencies and signify communication, visualization, and spirituality. Below is a brief overview of the seven main chakras.

## Root chakra

The root chakra emanates a bright red color and is located at the base of the spine, connecting to the adrenal gland. This symbolizes an individual's relationship with themselves and their connection to the Earth. Signifying a foundation, it pertains to basic survival needs such as safety, shelter, food, clothing, and a sense of belonging.

## Sacral chakra

The sacral chakra radiates an orange aura and is located directly below the belly button, connecting to the gonad gland. When viewing the physical body from head to toe, this chakra is in the exact center. It is connected to the sexual organs and the ability to experience pleasure. This chakra is where an individual expresses their sexuality and creativity but also where feelings of guilt and anger exist. These emotions relate to the nature of relationships and intimate interactions with others.

## Solar Plexus chakra

The solar plexus is a vibrant yellow color, is located several inches below the chest line, directly above the belly button, and connects to the pancreas gland. This chakra is associated with an individual's personal power and the connection to their community. It influences decision making ability, image, and personal accountability. Ultimately, it connects an individual's self-worth and confidence to the roles they uphold in society.

## Heart chakra

Connected to the thymus gland, the heart chakra emits a deep green color and is located in the center of the chest. This is exceptionally important as it links the higher spiritual chakras with the lower physical ones. It symbolizes altruism, acceptance, and self-love. Additionally, this chakra holds the ability to give and receive forgiveness.

## Throat chakra

The throat chakra exudes a turquoise aura and is located at the jugular to control communication. It is connected to the thyroid gland. This pertains to the ability to listen and receive external information as well as honestly articulating thoughts, feelings, and needs. It is associated with an individual's willpower, self-expression and authenticity.

## Third Eye chakra

The third eye chakra is the color of indigo and is located between the eyebrows. It's connected to the pituitary and pineal glands. This chakra creates an attachment between humans and their purpose in the physical world. It poses the questions, "Who am I mentally?" and "What is my vision in life?" It is responsible for the sixth sense, which is the connection to intuition, visualization, discernment, and self-reflection.

## Crown chakra

The crown chakra radiates a violet aura and is located at the top of the skull. It links the pineal gland to your higher self. This chakra controls the functions of the brain and central nervous system. It is harnessed to connect to your spirituality and higher power, while also responsible for your level of consciousness, belief systems and enlightenment.

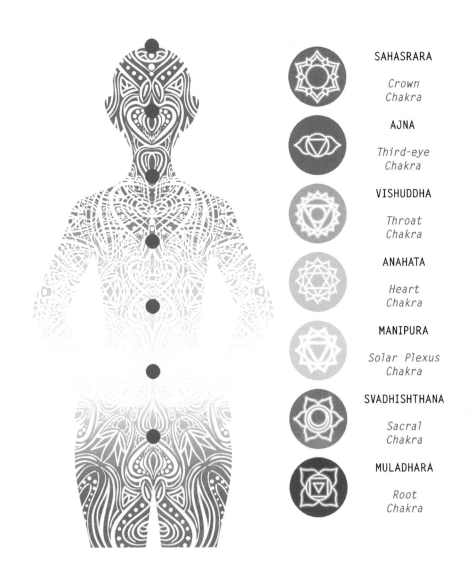

SAHASRARA

*Crown
Chakra*

AJNA

*Third-eye
Chakra*

VISHUDDHA

*Throat
Chakra*

ANAHATA

*Heart
Chakra*

MANIPURA

*Solar Plexus
Chakra*

SVADHISHTHANA

*Sacral
Chakra*

MULADHARA

*Root
Chakra*

# How to Work with Each Chakra

Having grasped the history of the chakra system and how these centers filter energy throughout the human body, it is paramount to understand how each chakra impacts the body and spirit. The following chapters thoroughly explain the relationship each chakra sustains on our physical, emotional, and spiritual health. The breakdown of each chakra shares information on how to examine if one is blocked, offering various tools to holistically heal it.

There is a detailed list for each chakra describing various physical and emotional signs of imbalance. Exploring this list leads to honest self-evaluation — pivotal in the activation process. Read the list and truthfully acknowledge if you engage in any of the behaviors or are living with any symptoms of a blocked chakra.

Once you have accepted a certain area of your life and sense a chakra is blocked, explore the different methods to strengthen it. There are various mindfulness practices simple enough to incorporate into your busiest days. The yoga asanas, essential oils, affirmations, crystals, and smoothie recipes will support your physical and emotional body in cycling through stagnant energy being retained in the chakra. Additionally, there is a grocery list full of healthy foods specifically supporting each chakra as well as healthy habits you can engage in going forward to prevent any future blockages.

The seven chakras are interrelated and once a lower chakra is in balance, it creates an opportunity to activate the next one. Dive into the breakdown of each chakra and examine which imbalances you may be experiencing at this moment in your life. Explore the holistic approaches to healing the chakra currently blocked. Implement any suggestion that resonates with you and incorporate it into your daily routine.

# Working with the Root Chakra

### Muladhara "Support"

### Relationship to the Self

### Associated with the *need for survival* & is blocked by **fear**

## Signs of a root chakra imbalance

- ❂ Constant lethargy and fatigue
- ❂ Feeling disassociated from your body
- ❂ Self-loathing or hatred towards your body
- ❂ Feeling abandoned or neglected by friends and family
- ❂ Feeling insecure in your home, work environment, or relationships
- ❂ Living in constant fear feeling you will lose your home, business, relationship, or personal belongings
- ❂ Exceptionally disorganized, constantly losing important items, and have difficulty staying organized
- ❂ Obsessively attached to other people and reliant on their energy to help
- ❂ Difficulty making decisions
- ❂ Persistent financial problems
- ❂ Excessive gambling habits and failing to treat your money with respect
- ❂ Consistently voicing your money problems to receive sympathy
- ❂ An intense fear of scarcity and an inability to spend money
- ❂ Experiencing chronic stress based on external circumstances [for example:  other people's behavior, the economy, or the weather]

## Symptoms associated with the root chakra

- ❂ Colitis
- ❂ Constipation
- ❂ Diverticulitis
- ❂ Obesity
- ❂ Irritable bowel syndrome
- ❂ Hemorrhoids
- ❂ Bladder infections
- ❂ Bursitis
- ❂ Rheumatoid arthritis
- ❂ Sciatica
- ❂ Eczema
- ❂ Fibromyalgia
- ❂ Plantar fasciitis
- ❂ Achilles tendinitis
- ❂ Alopecia

## Tools for the root chakra

Utilize these holistic tools to help energize and heal your root chakra:

**Stones:** ruby, moss agate, smokey quartz, bloodstone

**Oils:** cedar, cypress, clove

## Root chakra grocery list items

Root Vegetables:

- Sweet potatoes
- Carrots
- Beets
- Onions
- Garlic
- Radishes
- Butternut squash
- Acorn squash
- Pumpkin

Dense sources of protein:

- Eggs
- Meat products
- Fish
- Lentils
- Beans

Spices:

- Paprika
- Crushed red pepper
- Chives
- Ginger

Tea:

- Dandelion root tea

# Healthy Smoothie Recipe
## Beet Ya To It
## Apple Ginger BeetRoot Smoothie

## Ingredients:

- 1/2 cup of both ice and water
- 1 small raw beet
- 1 medium red apple
- 1 teaspoon of fresh ginger root
- 5 leaves of fresh mint
- Frozen strawberries or raspberries *optional*

## Instructions:

1. Begin with washing all produce.
2. Cut the beet, apple, ginger, and carrots into small sections. Do not remove the peel from these ingredients as they are all safe to digest and contain beneficial nutrients for your body.
3. Place the ice in the blender first, then add all of the ingredients and any other additives you desire.
4. Top with water. Blend until smooth and enjoy.

## Yoga asanas

Spend an average of 90 seconds in each posture. Prioritize breathwork and find a pattern of even inhalation and exhalation through both nostrils. Focus on flexing every muscle as you deepen the connection between your mind and body.

Child's Pose [Balasana]- hips push back to the heels.

Balasana variation - lift the palms and push down through the fingers for deeper shoulder stretch.

Puppy pose [Uttana Shishosana]- hips stay on top of the knees to simultaneously stretch the upper shoulders and hips.

Lizard [Utthan Pristhasana] - walk the foot towards the edge of the mat to focus on a deep hip flexor stretch.

Lizard variation [Utthan Pristhasana] - actively use your arm to deepen the stretch in hip flexor.

Lizard variation [Utthan Pristhasana] - actively use your arm to deepen the stretch in hip flexor.

Lizard variation [Utthan Pristhasana] - bring both elbows, or shoulders if your hip will allow, to deepen the stretch.

Toe stand variation [Padangusthasana] - play around with balancing on the balls of your feet.

Toe stand variation [Padangusthasana]- Kneeling toe stand with eagle arms to improve balance and concentration.

Seated wide legged forward fold [Upavistha Konasana] - flex the feet and rotate inner thighs up to the sky. Lean forward at the hips before rounding through the shoulders.

Seated wide legged forward fold [Upavistha Konasana] - flex the feet and rotate inner thighs up to the sky. Lean forward at the hips before rounding through the shoulders.

Supported Upavistha Konasana with a block - this variation is recommended for tighter hips as it allows more space for the body to stretch forward.

Bridge [Setu Bandha Sarvāṅgāsana] - keep the knees above the ankles and lift the pelvic floor to the sky.

Butterfly [Baddha Konasana] - bring the feet together and open the knees wide as you fold forward at the hips.

Seated forward fold [Paschimottanasana] - fold at the hips leading with the heart before rounding through the shoulders.

## Healthy habits that support your root chakra

Simplify and organize the chaos of your external environment to become more grounded within yourself.

- ❀ Organize your financial life:
    - ❀ Understand that disorganization leads to forgetfulness and creates opportunity for error. Lack of organization can contribute to extra or unnecessary expenses to fix any mistakes or accidents. Be meticulous and organize your life.
    - ❀ Prioritize your financial responsibilities by acknowledging any negative habits, insecurities, or fears regarding fiscal matters. Contact a trusted friend or financial advisor with any questions you may have.
    - ❀ Take pride in your investments and consciously manage your financial responsibilities.
    - ❀ Do not avoid any small charge that could evolve into a bigger problem if left unattended. Pay off that thirty-dollar parking ticket immediately, transfer your friend the money you owe them when they ask, and send your rent money a day before it is due.
    - ❀ Pay off any outstanding debt by creating a payment plan for your incomplete charges. Adhere to this plan.
    - ❀ Calculate every expense in your life and notice how you choose to spend your holiday fund.
    - ❀ Save ten percent of your income.
- ❀ Declutter your personal space:
    - ❀ Organize your closet by gathering all the clothes that do not suit your personality or make you feel confident. Donate them.
    - ❀ Clean your home, kitchen, car and office space. Remove all clutter and unnecessary items that do not add value to your current lifestyle.
- ❀ Document important upcoming dates:
    - ❀ Utilizing an agenda or Google calendar is pivotal in becoming grounded in yourself and diligent about personal/ professional commitments.

❀ Set reminders for when your credit bill is due, the date of your child's dance recital, your best friend's birthday, and when your car is up for a maintenance check. Always be one step ahead of yourself to avoid any crisis or stress.

❀ Ground yourself by connecting with nature:

❀ Spending time outdoors is exceptionally beneficial for healing the root chakra. Connecting with the earth helps calm the mind and balance the physical body by stabilizing the body's natural circadian rhythms.

❀ Explore local trails, rivers, reservoirs, and walking paths in your community. Walking is a great opportunity for practicing breathwork and allows time for self-reflection and evaluation of your current lifestyle.

❀ Walk barefoot as often as you can. Walking barefoot on dirt, mud, grass, sand, or leaves is invigorating for the body and mind as it stimulates increased blood flow while reducing inflammation.

❀ Find a new trail each week until you discover a spot that brings you true tranquility. Pay attention to your surroundings and notice how nature evolves around you. Use the colors, scents, and sounds of natural to stabilize the mind and increase the flow of energy through the physical and emotional body.

### *Affirmations to balance your root chakra*

*I trust myself and am grounded in my body.*
*This body is my home and I am safe here.*

*I have emotional and financial abundance*
*and will never go without. I am wealthy and*
*I will always have everything I need.*

*I am confident and secure that all of*
*my needs are provided for.*

# Working with the Sacral Chakra

### Svadhistana "Sweetness"

### Connection to creativity

Connected to the *experience of pleasure*
& is blocked by feelings of **guilt**

## Signs of a sacral chakra imbalance

❖ History of unsuccessful or unhealthy relationships

❖ Feeling abused, unloved, or hurt from experiencing sexual trauma

❖ Difficulty allowing yourself to be emotionally or sexually intimate

❖ Suppressing your sexual desires

❖ Experiencing shame or guilt around expressing your sexuality

❖ Inability to voice your sexual desires with your partner

❖ Relying solely on your sexuality to receive attention or admiration

❖ The inability to terminate unhealthy relationships

❖ Difficulty establishing boundaries in personal and professional relationships

❖ Intense feelings of guilt without valid explanation

❖ A fragile sense of self-worth

❖ Easily offended or hurt by the actions and words of others

❖ Lacking creativity in your life and constantly experiencing creative blocks

❖ Excessively consuming alcohol or using it for escapism

❖ Binge eating or starving yourself

❖ Excessive shopping habits

❖ Hoarding unused and insignificant items

## Symptoms associated with the sacral chakra

❖ Kidney problems

❖ Urinary tract infection

❖ Sexually transmitted diseases

❖ Candida

❖ Gout

❖ Menstrual problems

❖ PCOS

❖ Ovarian cysts

❖ Fibroids

❖ Bed wetting

❖ Erectile dysfunction

❖ Frigidity

❖ Hypersexuality or hyposexuality

❖ Generalized anxiety disorder

- Post-traumatic stress disorder
- Anorexia
- Bulimia
- Binge eating disorder
- Obsessive compulsive disorder
- Alcoholism
- Drug dependency

## Tools for the sacral chakra

Utilize these holistic tools to help energize and heal your sacral chakra:

**Stones:** sunstone, orange moonstone, orange calcite, obsidian

**Oils:** cardamon, orange, ylang ylang

## Solar plexus chakra grocery list items

Sweet fruits:

- Strawberries
- Raspberries
- Oranges
- Melons
- Mangos
- Passionfruit
- Coconut

Spices:

- Honey [manuka honey is highly recommended]
- Cinnamon
- Cardamon
- Vanilla

Teas:

- Vanilla honey
- Echinacea
- Hibiscus
- Cinnamon

# Healthy Smoothie Recipe

Can You Peel the Love Tonight?
Healthy Orange Julius Smoothie

## Ingredients:

- ½ cup of both ice and water
- Zest of 1 whole orange
- 1 whole orange, peeled
- 1 frozen banana
- ½ cup of plain greek yogurt
- 1 tablespoon of chia, flax, or hemp meal
- 2 teaspoons of vanilla extract
- Optional: frozen mango or papaya. 1 teaspoon of honey, maple syrup, or agave

## Instructions:

1. Using the small side of a cheese grater, zest the entire orange and set it aside. Peel and cut the banana and orange into small sections.

2. Place the ice at the bottom of the blender and then add the orange and banana chunks on top. Add the greek yogurt and then finish with the vanilla extract, protein seeds of your choosing, and orange zest. Add any extra options you fancy.

3. Top with water. Blend till smooth and enjoy.

## Yoga asanas

Spend an average of 90 seconds in each posture. Prioritize breathwork and find a pattern of even inhalation and exhalation through both nostrils. Focus on flexing every muscle as you deepen the connection between your mind and body.

Yogi squat [malasana]- ground through the feet and keep the heart and head high as the hips lower below the knees. Elbows can be used to open the knees wide to deepen the stretch in the hips.

Supported malasana with a block - focus on keeping a strong back and avoid rounding through the shoulders.

Reclined butterfly [supta baddha konasana] - bring the feet together and open the knees wide. Recline the upper body and allow gravity to work its magic on your knees to activate the hips.

Reclined butterfly [supta baddha konasana] - bring the feet together and open the knees wide. Recline the upper body and allow gravity to work its magic on your knees to activate the hips.

Extended mountain pose [Utthita Hasta in Tadasana] - activate the hips by taking a slight back bed in standing mountain pose. Gently look behind you and elongate the neck bringing the shoulders back as well.

Camel [Ustrasana] - begin by kneeling with the hips directly above the knees. Use your hands to push the hips forward so the upper body can recline backwards.

Camel [Ustrasana] - Drop the hands behind the feet as you continue to push the hips forward.

Camel [Ustrasana]- walk the hands to the heels if your hips and spine will allow.

Camel [Ustrasana]- walk the hands to the heels if the flexibility in your hips and spine will allow. Continue to lift through the hips and heart.

Half split [Ardha Hanumanasana] - take this hamstring stretch as gentle or as deep as your body calls for. Flexing the foot allows for a deeper stretch in the intended hamstring.

Standing wide hip circles to loosen the sacral:

Extend the pelvis and hip bones forward, loosening the abdomen.

Rotate hips to the right.

Continue to circle the hips backwards as you flex the abdomen and tuck belly button to the back of the spine.

Slowly bring the hips to the left, loosening the core.

Finish the circle by bringing the hips forward. Repeat three times in each direction.

Standing wide legged forward fold [Prasarita Padottanasana] - bend at the waist taking this as deep as the hips will allow.

Prasarita Padottanasana variation with additional shoulder stretch - interlace the fingers at the base of the spine and lift the hands to stretch through the shoulders.

Half pigeon [Ardha Kapotasana] - bring the knee to the edge of the mat with toes pointed toward the opposite side. Lift the chest and elongate the spine before folding over at the hips. Keep your weight evenly distributed over both hips.

Half pigeon [Ardha Kapotasana]-bring the knee to the edge of the mat with toes pointed toward the opposite side. Lift the chest and elongate the spine before folding over at the hips. Keep your weight evenly distributed over both hips.

Supported Ardha Kapotasana with a block - use a block or a pillow to help keep the hips aligned.

Supported Ardha Kapotasana with a block - use a block or a pillow to help keep the hips aligned.

## Healthy habits that support your sacral chakra

Acknowledge the things bringing you pleasure and engage in these activities more frequently.

- ✿ Move your body:

  - ❊ Begin every morning with large hip circles to loosen your pelvic floor muscles. Five wide, elongated circles will suffice. These can be done while your coffee is brewing, in the shower as your hair conditioner is setting, or while you are brushing your teeth.
  - ❊ Get creative. Dance, run, jog, swim, twerk, stretch, paint, sew, free draw, fish, bake or ride a bike. Do one thing a day that brings your body pleasure.
  - ❊ Finish the day with a gentle pelvic floor stretch. Supported frog, reclined butterfly, or wide legged forward fold can all be done in bed if you had a long day.

- ✿ Expand your sexual horizon:

  - ❊ Experience an orgasm without the use of a sex toy or pornography. Love and pleasure yourself without any external influences to help deepen the relationship with your body.
  - ❊ Explore Tantric sex and practice it with your partner.
  - ❊ Create a peaceful space for sexual intercourse using candles, incense, or calming music.
  - ❊ Do not rush. Value the beauty of sex, your body, and your partner's as you focus on the giving and receiving of pleasure.

- ✿ Evaluate your healthy and destructive habits:

  - ❊ Reflect on your eating, drinking, and shopping habits. Notice when you overeat, binge on sweets, abuse alcohol, or aimlessly shop to ease or avoid anxious feelings.
  - ❊ Examine how you typically attract your romantic partners. Review past relationships and determine if you connected with your significant other emotionally and intellectually or if it was predominantly sexual. Acknowledge how your relationships impacted your emotional health and set an intention for the type of relationship and partner you would like to manifest.

❖ Seek professional and spiritual support:

❀ There is a branch of therapy for every area of life. There is a spiritual healer, sex therapist, trauma therapist, or relationship therapist [and countless others] in your city or town who can offer support through any roadblock. Acknowledge any feelings of guilt, difficulties setting boundaries, or intimacy complications and discuss these with a trusted professional. Implement the advice they offer and reflect on any progress made.

### *Affirmations to balance your sacral chakra*

*I allow myself to receive all of life's pleasures. I am confident in my sexuality and am open to intimacy.*

*I consciously balance my desires and allow creative energy to flow to and through me.*

*I connect well with others without losing who I am and give graciously without failing to meet my own needs.*

# Working with the Solar Plexus Chakra

### Manipura "Lustrous gem"

### Connection to your personal power

### Associated with *willpower* & is blocked by shame and insecurity

## Signs of a solar plexus chakra imbalance

- Low self-worth and excessive negative self-talk
- A lack of enthusiasm in your personal and professional life
- Experiencing career burnout
- Unable to relax and consistently experiencing anxiety
- Difficulty taking action on your visions or goals
- Living with a "victim" mindset and consistently creating excuses for your lack of success
- Relentlessly needing to "be right" when conversing with your partner or companions
- Seeking validation from external sources for your lifestyle choices
- Minimizing your voice and avoiding confrontation to "keep the peace" in relationships
- Quickly agreeing with statements or situations that do not resonate with you due to a lack of confidence in voicing your opinion
- Feeling ashamed for who you are and the belief systems you hold
- Inability to accept feedback or constructive criticism
- Responding to advice or an alternative perspective with aggravation and impatience
- Downplaying any milestone fearing your success will intimidate others
- Purposefully ignoring your intuition
- Prone to digestive problems, experiencing irregular bowel movements, or an living with an excessive amount of food allergies

## Symptoms associated with the solar plexus chakra

- Generalized anxiety disorder
- Depression
- Gastroesophageal Reflux Disease [GERD]
- Jaundice
- Diarrhea
- Constipation
- Acid reflux
- Heartburn
- Indigestion

- Diabetes
- Blood sugar disorders
- Liver infection
- Gallstones
- Celiac disease
- Crohn's disease
- Pancreatitis
- Stomach ulcers
- Cystic acne
- Shingles
- Psoriasis
- Inflammatory bowel disease
- Feeling bloated

## Tools for the solar plexus chakra

Utilize these holistic tools to help energize and heal your solar plexus chakra:

**Stones:** citrine, yellow topaz, malachite, tiger's eye

**Oils:** chamomile, lemon, thyme

## Solar plexus chakra grocery list items

Fibrous grains and seeds:

- Quinoa
- Rice
- Buckwheat
- Granola
- Flax seeds
- Chia seeds

Spices:

- Ginger
- Chamomile
- Turmeric
- Cumin
- Fennel

Tea:

- Ginger lemon tea
- Peppermint tea
- Gentian root

# Healthy Smoothie Recipe

Always On Holiday
Nourishing Miami Vice
Healthy Pina Colada

Ingredients:

- ½ cup of both ice and water
- ½ cup of frozen pineapple
- ½ cup of condensed coconut milk

## Healthy Strawberry Daiquiri

Ingredients:

- ½ cup of both ice and water
- 1 cup of frozen strawberries
- 1 tablespoon of lime juice
- 2 teaspoons of agave or stevia sweetener

Instructions:

These smoothies are enjoyable to drink separately, but compliment each other exceptionally well and can be prepared together.

1. Add the ice first followed by the pineapple, strawberries, coconut milk, lime juice, and sweetener.

2. Top with water and blend until smooth.

These measurements yield enough for two servings. Share with a partner or treat yourself to a second round. While drinking this smoothie, envision yourself relaxing in a cabana with your friends during golden hour at South Beach. Acknowledge something about yourself you are proud of. Bring these vibes into the rest of your day.

## Yoga asanas

Spend an average of 90 seconds in each posture. Prioritize breathwork and find a pattern of even inhalation and exhalation through both nostrils. Focus on flexing every muscle as you deepen the connection between your mind and body.

Warrior I [Virabhadrasana I] - stand with both hips facing forward, the back foot at a forty-five degree angle, and the front knee over the front ankle. Lift through the abdomen and bring the upper arms up to your ears. This is a very active asana so it is important to flex every muscle in your body while focusing the energy on balancing with a strong core.

Warrior II [Virabhadrasana II] - bend front knee over ankle, set back foot at a ninety degree angle, and open both the hips and shoulders to the side. Lift through the abdomen, bringing the belly button to the spine, open the arms so the hands are inline with each other, and continue to sink the hips lower with every exhale.

Warrior II [Virabhadrasana II] - bend front knee over ankle, set back foot at a ninety degree angle, and open both the hips and shoulders to the side. Lift through the abdomen, bringing the belly button to the spine, open the arms so the hands are inline with each other, and continue to sink the hips lower with every exhale.

Reverse warrior [Viparita Virabhadrasana] - flip the front palm and flow the arm backwards taking a slight backbend to stretch through the obliques.

Warrior III [Virabhadrasana III] - evenly distribute your weight on the standing foot and embrace the core while kicking through the back foot. It is important to focus your concentration on one point and keep the abdomen activated the entire time to stabilize the body.

Supported Virabhadrasana III - place hands on hips to stabilize the core and improve concentration.

Extended side angle [Utthita Parsvakonasana]- from warrior II transition the upper body towards the front leg and lower the arm towards the ankle. Continue to open the hips, heart and shoulders to the side.

Goddess [Utkata Konasana]- with your weight evenly distributed over both feet, lower the knees over the ankles keeping the core braced and the spine long.

Crescent low lunge [Anjaneyasana]- keep both legs in their separate lane and frame the front foot with both hands as you activate the core.

Crescent high lunge [Ashta Chandrasana]- transition from low crescent lunge to high lunge by using the core to lift you upright. Lift through the abdomen and lower the hips with each exhale.

Table top [Bharmanasana]- bring the shoulders over wrists and hips over knees while keeping the head in line with neck and a straight spine.

Cow pose [Bitilasana]- transitioning from table top, lift hips high while simultaneously curving the spine and lifting chin and heart to the sky.

Cat pose [Marjariasana]- transitioning from cow pose, use your breath to round through the shoulders and tuck the hips. Bring the belly button to the spine as it curves in the opposite direction. Focus on even breathwork here.

## Healthy habits that support your solar plexus

Remove all things that physically and emotionally aggravate your gut health.

- Prioritize gut health by improving diet and digestion:

    - Honestly assess your nutritional habits and acknowledge any detrimental eating patterns.
    - Schedule an appointment with a registered dietician, nutritionist or naturopath to explore how to consume nutritionally dense food you enjoy eating.
    - Invest in a blood test to discover any food allergies or intolerances you may have.
    - Seek advice from a professional on methods for avoiding any foods that aggravate and inflame the gut.

- Experience Colon Hydrotherapy:

    - Colon irrigation gently flushes the colon of accumulated toxins, worms, parasites, or any waste the body is retaining. On average, a colonic takes 45 to 50 minutes and helps remove waste the body cannot release naturally while strengthening the digestive tract and restabilizing gut health.
    - Research trustworthy colon irrigation therapists in your city or town to find one you connect with. Explore their services and examine how your body and spirit responds to the cleanse. Invest in monthly colonics if this form of therapy resonates with you.

- Create a moral code that you confidently uphold:

    - Become a person of integrity who lives up to their word. When you make an intention to do something, become something, or create something — follow through with it. You build trust with yourself and others when your actions match your words.
    - Pay attention to any hypocritical behaviors in yourself. If you are going to judge others for their actions and then proceed to engage in the same behaviors, it will be difficult to build a set of behavioral standards for yourself.
    - Establishing a set of moral codes and daily habits you inherently follow contributes to your overall character. Think about the person

you want to be and act as him or her. Set intentions and create habits that uphold the integrity of this desired person. Building a sturdy character and living up to your character's reputation creates a strong foundation within yourself and in the role you play in society.

Strengthen your self-esteem:

- Do the "Mirror Challenge" for 21 days straight. Look at yourself directly in the mirror and iterate seven positive qualities you love about yourself. These qualities can be physical or psychological attributes and can be repeated over the course of the challenge. It is simply an internal conversation where you list seven magnificent qualities about yourself, for twenty-one days. It is not an easy challenge, but the results are profound. Stick with it.
- Accept constructive criticism from friends or colleagues and offer thanks for their honest opinion. Use this feedback to strengthen your confidence in your professional or personal relationships.
- Acknowledge what you are shameful of: Are you embarrassed of your relationship, living arrangements, career choices, or physical appearance? Admit to yourself where you feel shame and work to improve those areas of your life.
- Do not compare yourself to others. Your journey — every challenge and accomplishment — is unique to you. People can act as sources of inspiration or reflection, but their journey should not be compared to yours. Remind yourself that you are on your own timeline and there is no energy for comparison.

### *Affirmations to balance your solar plexus*

*I openly step into my personal power and take
responsibility for everything that occurs in my life.*

*I live my life with purpose and am motivated
to pursue this purpose every day.*

*I own my life with conviction and
confidently make my own decisions.*

# Working with the Heart Chakra

### Anahata "Unstuck"

### Acceptance of unconditional love

### Deals with *Love* & is hindered by grief and envy

## Signs of a heart chakra imbalance

- Feeling unworthy of love
- Giving with the expectation of receiving and constantly looking for rewards
- Fearing romantic commitment
- Constantly seeking reassurance from your partner for why they love you
- Routinely searching for reasons to be angry and instigate fights with your partner
- Holding grudges against others and unwilling to offer forgiveness
- Overly critical of other people and their life choices
- Having a jealous nature
- Intense feelings of envy when your friends reach certain milestones
- Experiencing sorrow and depression while observing a happy relationship
- Holding intense grief related to death or a relationship ending
- Always taking care of others but neglecting your own physical and mental health
- Difficulty finding positive qualities about yourself and harshly judging yourself often
- Inability to forgive yourself for past mistakes
- Losing your sense of identity
- Difficulty breathing and experience shortness of breath

## Symptoms associated with the heart chakra

- High blood pressure
- Low blood pressure
- Hyperventilation
- Pulmonary hypertension
- Lethargy
- Pneumonia
- Shortness of breath
- Asthma
- Emphysema
- Dyspnea

- Panic attacks
- Chest pain
- Chronic obstructive pulmonary disease
- Cardiovascular diseases
- Nail biting
- Tremor

## Tools for the heart chakra

Utilize these holistic tools to help energize and heal your heart center:

**Stones:** rose quartz, emerald, green jade, rhodonite

**Oils:** rose, geranium, clary sage

## Heart chakra grocery list items

Cruciferous vegetables:

- Spinach
- Kale
- Arugula
- Collard greens
- Brussel sprouts
- Broccoli
- Cabbage
- Cauliflower
- Dandelion greens
- Bok choy
- Celery

Spices:

- Basil
- Thyme
- Cilantro

Teas:

- Green tea
- Black tea
- Rose tea

# Healthy smoothie recipe

## Green & Clear
## Green Apple Smoothie

Ingredients:

- ½ cup of both ice and water
- 1 whole granny smith apple
- 1 frozen banana
- ½ cup of frozen avocado
- 1 tablespoon of lemon juice
- Handful of spinach or kale
- Peeled kiwi *optional*

Instructions:

1. Add ice first.
2. Cut apple, banana, and avocado into small sections and add to the blender along with the greens. Top with lemon juice and water.
3. Blend until smooth and enjoy.
4. While sipping this smoothie, reflect on your favorite quality about yourself.

## Green Thumb Detox

Ingredients:

- ½ cup of both ice and water
- ½ cucumber
- 1 stalk of celery
- 1 medium sized red apple
- 5 mint leaves
- Handful of spinach or kale
- 1 tablespoon of lemon juice
- 1 teaspoon of agave or stevia
- Frozen avocado or peeled kiwi *optional*

Instructions:

1. Cleanse and dice the cucumber, celery, and apple. Add these ingredients with the mint and greens to the blender after the ice.
2. Top off with water, lemon juice, and your choice of sweetener.
3. Blend under smooth and enjoy.
4. While drinking this smoothie, acknowledge something you love about your partner or best friend. Then tell them.

## Yoga asanas

Spend an average of 90 seconds in each posture. Prioritize breathwork and find a pattern of even inhalation and exhalation through both nostrils. Focus on flexing every muscle as you deepen the connection between your mind and body.

> Cobra [Bhujangasana] - push through the hands and arms to bring the chest upward while simultaneously activating the lower spine.

> Baby cobra [Variation of Bhujangasana] - use this variation if full cobra is too intense for your lower back.  Keep elbows tucked tight to your sides, engage the core, and lift the chest forward.

Seal [Variation of Bhujangasana]- extend the arms beyond the shoulders to receive a different stretch for the lower back which helps open the heart center. The goal of this variation is to bring the hands into the far corners of the mat while keeping the body in a similar shape to cobra.

Upward facing dog [Urdhva Mukha Shvanasana] - transition to upward facing dog through cobra pose. Lift the legs off the mat and continue to push down through the hands as the chin lifts towards the sky for a deeper backbend.

Chair [Utkatasana] - bring the toes together with heels slightly apart. Bend the knees and sit the hips back while keeping the spine straight and the core engaged. Lift the chest high and keep the head in line with the neck.

Dancer [Natarajasana] - start from a standing position. Bend the leg and grip onto the inside of the ankle. Keep the chest high while you kick the leg backwards.

Natarajasana variation from table top - this variation is great for building strength and balance in the body. Focus on stretching through the chest while keeping your concentration on one spot.

Fish pose [Matsyasana] - make a triangle shape with the hands and place them at the base of your spine. Recline onto your elbows and bring the crown of your head down to the mat. Stretch through the neck while extending the chest up to the sky.

Supported Matsyasana - use one block between the shoulder blades to help lift the chest center towards the sky.

Supported Matsyasana with two blocks - Place one block under the head to protect the neck and the second placed between the shoulder blades lifting the chest center to the sky.

Triangle [Trikonasana]- prepare for triangle pose with warrior II legs. Keep heels, hips, shoulders, and hands in line as you open our chest center to the side.

Triangle [Trikonasana]

## Healthy habits that support your heart chakra

Find and list five things that you are grateful for every morning.

- Become a pro at offering forgiveness:

  - Accept someone's genuine apology when it is offered. They are human and navigating life just as you are.
  - Reflect on any person or event that has emotionally hurt you and caused you grief. Accept this grief.
  - Offer forgiveness to that person, even if you believe they are unworthy of forgiveness. This is about your healing process. Forgiving someone for their wrongdoing — whether through prayer, a drafted email, or a burned letter — supports your journey of detachment and spiritual growth.

- Acknowledge where you experience envy and transform this emotion in a positive manner:

  - The feeling of envy is when you want something that someone else currently possesses. This feeling can relate to desiring a certain career, mindset, relationship, income, or lifestyle you observe others experiencing.
  - Where you experience envy is what you innately desire for yourself.
  - When this emotion arises in the body, use it constructively. This can be a positive emotion for guiding you along your journey and creating goals for your life. As envy can be a rather personal emotion, use it in a positive sense of building and creating the life you desire, rather than negatively trying to rob others of their accomplishments.

- Think twice before passing judgment:

  - Notice how quickly you judge others based on their wardrobe, career, relationship, or lifestyle choices. No one knows your whole story and what you have overcome, so do not expect to know someone else's by one interaction.

✿ Be gentle with yourself:

- Practice self-love. Start with one small act of kindness each day — the "Mirror Challenge" will help here. Accept yourself as you are and then change anything you can control.
- Take accountability for the role you played in any toxic relationships, disputes, or friendship complications. Acknowledge your patterns and create a plan to avoid these detrimental behaviors in the future.
- Reflect on any past mistakes and forgive yourself for them. Take the lesson from it and move on.

## Affirmations to balance your heart chakra

*I accept and love myself as I am.*

*My heart is open to receiving. I share love with others unconditionally.*

*I offer forgiveness to those who have betrayed me. I forgive myself for past mistakes and absorb the lessons I have learned.*

# Working with the Throat Chakra

### Vissudha "Purification"

### Self-Expression

**Associated with the *truth* & is blocked by deception and dishonesty**

## Signs of a throat chakra imbalance

- Overwhelmingly anxious when public speaking
- Spreading and listening to gossip
- Constantly lying to your friends and loved ones
- Lying to yourself and failing to follow through with the intentions you set
- Hiding money, partying, or lifestyle choices from your partner
- Cheating on your partner or knowingly being involved in an affair
- Working for a company that does not align with your morals
- Staying in a relationship or career that fails to satisfy you
- Agreeing with others out of fear of voicing your opinion
- Feeling unworthy and believing that your voice and opinion do not matter
- Talking excessively and having poor listening skills
- Speaking harshly to others
- Quickly responding without processing your thoughts
- Failing to uphold your physical, mental, or spiritual needs
- Clenching your jaw and grinding your teeth

## Symptoms associated with the throat chakra

- Sore throat
- Flu
- Fevers
- Hay fever
- Laryngitis
- Swollen glands
- Speech disorders
- Hypothyroidism
- Hyperthyroidism
- Tonsillitis
- Toothaches
- Ear infections
- Tinnitus
- Neck pain
- Hiccups
- Mouth ulcers
- Shoulder stiffness

## Tools for the throat chakra

Utilize these holistic tools to help energize and heal your throat chakra:

**Stones:** blue lace agate, aquamarine, turquoise, angelite

**Oils:** lavender, sage, peppermint

## Throat chakra grocery list items

Hydrating fruit juices:

- Cucumber, mint, and lemon juice
- Celery juice
- Cantaloupe juice
- Fresh orange juice
- Fresh grapefruit juice

Teas:

- Anise tea
- Slippery elm tea
- Licorice root tea
- Marshmallow root tea
- Chamomile tea

# Healthy smoothie recipe

## Teal the Deal
## Blue Spirulina Mermaid Smoothie

Ingredients:

- ½ cup of ice
- 3/4 cup of almond milk or coconut milk
- 1 frozen banana
- ¼ cup frozen mango
- ¼ cup of frozen blueberries
- ½ teaspoon of blue spirulina
- 1 tablespoon of chia, flax, or hemp meal
- Slivered almonds or coconut shreds *optional*

Instructions:

1. Add ice to the blender, followed by the banana, mango, blueberries, and blue spirulina.

2. Finish with the protein seeds and milk of your choosing. The extra options can be added to the smoothie or used as a garnish.

3. Blend until smooth and enjoy.

## Yoga asanas

Spend an average of 90 seconds in each posture. Prioritize breathwork and find a pattern of even inhalation and exhalation through both nostrils. Focus on flexing every muscle as you deepen the connection between your mind and body.

> Wheel [Chakrasana] - start wheel pose from bridge. Flip palms over your shoulders so your fingers are pointed towards your heels. Push through the hands and feet as the hips lift to the sky. Look behind you to stretch through the neck.

Transitions to fallen triangle [Patita Tarasana]:

Downward facing dog

Three legged dog - kick leg high into the sky keeping the hips in line with each other.

Bend the knee and bring it into the chest as you squeeze your core tight.

Keep the arms in the same position as you extend the leg towards the opposite wrist.

Open the chest towards the front leg and lengthen the arm into the sky. Elongate through the neck as the hips continue to lift upwards.

Inversions:

Hips on a block - place a block or pillow at the base of the spine and lift the legs into the sky.

Shoulder stand [Sarvangasana] - use your arms and hands to support your hips so they can rise above the heart. Protect the neck by keeping the head straight and the chin tucked into the chest.

Leg variations in shoulder stand - stabilize the core and protect the neck before exploring different leg variations.

Plow [Halasana] - Let the legs extend all the way behind you keeping the arms long on the mat. Protect the neck by keeping the head straight and the chin tucked into the chest.

Caterpillar pose [Ashtanga namaskara] - begin from puppy pose. Bring the hands underneath the shoulders and place the chin on the mat. Look in front of you as the neck elongates and receives a deep stretch.

Humble warrior [Baddha Virabhadrasana] - begin from a warrior I pose. Interlace the fingers at the base of the spine and extend the arms to the sky as the upper body drops inside the front knee. Let the head and neck release down.

## Healthy habits to strengthen your throat chakra

Have pride in your voice and authentically communicate with yourself and others.

- Embody your truth:
  - Drop your Ego and acknowledge what makes you truly happy.
  - Be honest with the personal and professional lifestyle you wish to live.
  - Work a job you love, date a person you love, eat food you love, and spend your time doing things you love.

- Practice integrity in every area of your life:
  - Always speak your honest opinion when someone asks. Do not withhold the truth at the risk of offending others.
  - Admit when you have made a mistake and do not project any responsibility on anyone else. Do not lie to avoid confrontation or punishment.
  - Hold secrets in confidence when others ask it of you.
  - Avoid spreading and listening to gossip. Do not build friendships on the foundation of gossip and refrain from searching for it.
  - Be faithful to your partner. Do not cheat or find reasons to justify any inappropriate behavior.

- Strengthen your communication skills:
  - Engage in meaningful conversations.
  - Listen before you speak. Allow someone to process all of their thoughts before you respond.
  - Ask before you offer advice. Often people do not want advice, they simply need space to freely speak their thoughts.
  - Process your thoughts thoroughly before you vocalize them. Clear thoughts produce effective conversations.

- Dedicate days for silence:
  - Balance your throat chakra by practicing silence and resting your voice.

- Dedicate several hours a week or a full day for a silent retreat. Refrain from listening to music, checking social media, answering calls, and chatting with strangers.
- Inform your friends, colleagues, and clients of your intentions before turning your phone off and enjoying quality time for solitude.
- Rest your voice, observe your surroundings, and choose not to react to any situation that will compromise your sacred moments of silence.

## *Affirmations to open your throat chakra*

*I express myself clearly. I am a strong communicator
and confidently speak with honest intentions.*

*My voice is important. There is validity in my statements.*

*I am honest with myself and the world.
I speak and live my truth.*

# Working with the Third Eye Chakra

Anja "Perception" or "Knowledge"

Connection to Intuition and Intellect Associated
with *insight* & blocked by illusion

## Signs of a third eye chakra imbalance

- Difficulty and doubt around making decisions
- Trouble trusting yourself and always relying on the opinions of others before making a decision
- Disconnection from your intuition
- Ignoring life lessons by reliving past mistakes
- Struggling to find a purpose in life
- Feeling confused and spiritually lost
- Asking the question, "Why am I here?" frequently and being overly curious about the meaning of life
- Having a weak memory
- Difficulty concentrating on your tasks
- Intense and consistent headaches
- Impaired vision

## Symptoms associated with the third eye chakra

- Tension headaches
- Paranoia
- Vertigo
- Blindness
- Astigmatism
- Macular degeneration
- Glaucoma
- Cataract
- Styes
- Deafness
- Earaches
- Sinus problems
- Diabetic retinopathy
- Fear
- Manic depression
- Dyslexia
- Sleep disorders
- Nightmares
- Equilibrium imbalances

## Tools for the third eye chakra

Utilize these holistic tools to help energize and heal your third eye chakra:

**Stones:** lapis lazuli, opal, sodalite, labradorite

**Oils:** jasmine, rosemary, patchouli

## Third eye chakra grocery list items

Dark blue or purple fruits:

- Blueberries
- Blackberries
- Passionfruit
- Red grapes
- Red cherries

Juices:

- Tart cherry juice
- Organic grape juice

Teas:

- Peppermint tea
- Mugwort tea

# Healthy smoothie recipe

### That's Berry Sweet of You
### Mixed Berry and Mint Smoothie

Ingredients:

- ½ cup of both ice and water
- 1 frozen banana
- ½ cup of frozen mixed berries
- 5 fresh mint leaves
- Handful of spinach or kale
- 1 tablespoon of chia, flax or hemp meal
- Can substitute frozen avocado for banana *optional*

Instructions:

1. Add ice first. Then combine the banana, mixed berries, greens, and protein seeds of your choosing.

2. Top with water and blend until smooth.

3. While enjoying this smoothie remind yourself of your purpose. Acknowledge the value you bring to yourself and the world when you live out this purpose.

## Yoga asanas

Spend an average of 90 seconds in each posture. Prioritize breathwork and find a pattern of even inhalation and exhalation through both nostrils. Focus on flexing every muscle as you deepen the connection between your mind and body.

Standing forward fold [Uttanasana] - evenly distribute your weight over both feet and bend forward at the waist. Bend your knees as deeply as needed to bring your forehead to your knees.

Gorilla [Padahastasana] - Place each hand under the feet, palms facing upward. Let the head and neck release down as you straighten the arms, simultaneously receiving a deep shoulder stretch.

Eagle [Garudasana] - Begin this pose from chair pose. Lift one leg and cross it over the other, while twisting the same arm under the opposite. Keep your focus concentrated on one spot as you find your balance.

Stork Bird [Saaras Pakshi] - lift one leg to a ninety-degree angle and explore any leg variations here while keeping your eyes concentrated on one spot and core engaged the entire time.

Pyramid [Parsvottanasana] - keep the heels in line as the front toes point forward and the back toes pointed at a forty-five degree angle. Ensure the hips stay in line as you fold forward and bring the forehead to the knee. Let the head and neck release down allowing for fresh blood to flow to the head.

Pyramid [Parsvottanasana]

Dolphin [ardha pincha mayurasana] - start dolphin from downward facing dog. Bend the knees and lower each elbow to the ground while keeping the palms flat.

Dolphin [ardha pincha mayurasana] - Allow the head and neck to relax down as you straighten the legs and stretch through the shoulders.

## Healthy habits to help support your third eye

Look beyond the surface and question everything you read and see.

- ❁ Strengthen your intuition:

  - ❁ Question everything you hear or read by inquiring if there is a deeper meaning or lesson behind it. There often is.
  - ❁ Before acting on an idea, making a decision, or reacting to an event, assess the situation from several different perspectives. There may be another perspective or outlook that could help strengthen the outcome. Write a pros/cons list and evaluate all areas prior to committing to a decision.
  - ❁ Any inspiration or message you receive is your intuition speaking through you. Pay attention to these messages and trust them. Depending on the message you receive, it may be channeled through your third eye and then projected out another chakra. Regardless of where your body receives this intuition, any feeling, idea, or motivation is meant to be acknowledged. Listen and trust the voice in your head and feeling in your gut. It will guide you to find the direction you need to go.

- ❁ Protect your subconscious mind:

  - ❁ Filter the information you read and watch, remember your subconscious mind retains everything it sees.
  - ❁ Notice how much time you spend on social media and take frequent breaks from constantly scrolling on all platforms.
  - ❁ Pay attention to the people you follow and use discernment when absorbing any new information. Do not believe everything you read.
  - ❁ The last fifteen minutes before falling asleep and the first fifteen minutes upon waking up are crucial moments to mold your subconscious mind — use this time wisely.

- ❁ Enjoy the sunshine and practice sungazing:

  - ❁ The pineal gland requires sunlight to efficiently function and it is crucial to receive daily sunlight as it energizes the body and mind.

❀ Sungazing is a practice of gradually introducing sunlight to your eyes during sunrise and sunset when the sun is at the lowest ultraviolet-index times of the day. The techniques of this ancient practice have been used in various cultures such as Tibetan, Aztec, Indian yoga, Mayan and Egyptian to energize the mind, heal the physical body, and increase telepathic skills.

❀ Sungazing should be done an hour after sunrise or an hour before sunset and standing barefoot on dirt, grass, or sand. Stand tall and practice even nostril breathing as you stare directly into the sun for ten seconds. Stop after ten seconds. **It is crucial to follow these details to protect your eyesight.**

❀ As you continue to grow your practice and strengthen your pineal gland you can expand on the amount of time you sun gaze by five to ten seconds each day.

❀ See the world through a new pair of eyes every single day:

❀ Keep your mentality fresh. Whenever you are about to do something, act as if it is the first time you have ever done it. Practice this even if you have been following the same routine for years on end. For example, imagine you are drinking a new coffee order at a new cafe right before your first shift at a new job. You intend on finishing the day with a new workout class at the gym you recently joined. You may have been drinking the same coffee, made by the same barista, at the cafe right outside your office and training at the same gym for the past several years. Nonetheless, imagining everything is a new experience when you partake in it keeps you mentally stimulated and constantly intrigued with the world around you.

## Affirmations to open your third eye chakra

*I have a strong intuition and confidently follow it.*

*I have a clear vision of my purpose on earth and use the insight provided to me as guidance.*

*I am aware of myself and recognize wisdom comes from within. Everything I need for success is already inside of me.*

# Working with the Crown Chakra

**Sahasrara "Thousand-petaled"**

**Relationship to Spirituality**

Connected to *celestial energy* & hindered by attachment and the Ego

## Signs of a crown chakra imbalance

- Believing the world wants you to fail
- Strong attachment to material objects
- Defining yourself by your material possessions and prioritizing your "image"
- Difficulty sleeping or suffering severe night terrors
- A fear of doing things on your own
- Loneliness or aimlessness
- Emotional distress
- Disconnected from your friends and family
- A weak connection to a higher power
- Searching for answers outside of yourself
- Feeling triggered by those who are connected to spirituality
- Feeling unworthy of divine intervention or that your higher power has abandoned you

## Symptoms associated with the crown chakra

- Chronic migraines
- Amnesia and senility
- Confusion
- Neuralgia
- Vertigo
- Fatigue
- Insomnia
- Fibromyalgia
- Alopecia
- Paralysis
- Epilepsy
- Parkinson's disease
- Depression
- Dissociative identity disorder
- Schizophrenia
- Neurosis
- Psychosis
- Multiple Sclerosis

## Tools for the crown chakra

Utilize these holistic tools to help energize and heal your crown chakra:

**Stones:** amethyst, topaz, clear quartz, tourmaline

**Oils:** frankincense, rosewood, sandalwood

Fasting and detoxing are highly recommended in a healthy and controlled manner to develop the crown chakra. Experiment with intermittent fasting, a fresh juice cleanse at the beginning of a new moon or full moon cycle, or a 24-hour fast once a month.

The crown chakra is energized by meditation and prayer. Abstaining from food for a significant period of time helps activate the flow of energy to the crown. Speak to your spiritual healer and doctor before implementing these practices into your lifestyle to assess whether they will suit your current mental and physical health.

These practices, when done properly, positively activate the crown chakra as they help awaken the highest form of spiritual communication.

## Crown chakra grocery list items

Teas:

- Lavender tea
- Periwinkle Tea
- White Peony Tea

Incense smudging herbs to purify your spaces of living:

- Sage
- White sage
- Copal
- Myrrh
- Juniper
- Lavender
- Frankincense

# Healthy smoothie recipe

## There are a Million Reeses to Smile
## Espresso Peanut Butter Cup Smoothie

Ingredients:

- ½ cup of both ice and water
- 1 serving of vanilla protein [any brand of vegan protein is recommended]
- 1 frozen banana
- 2 tablespoons of peanut butter
- 2 teaspoons of cacao powder
- 1 teaspoon of instant coffee
- 1 tablespoon of chia, flax, or hemp meal
- Dashes of cinnamon

Instructions:

1. Add ice. Combine all ingredients.

2. Top with water. Blend until smooth.

3. Sprinkle extra cinnamon on top and enjoy.

4. Smile. Remind yourself that this life on Earth is very brief and meant to be enjoyed.

## Yoga asanas

Spend an average of 90 seconds in each posture. Prioritize breathwork and find a pattern of even inhalation and exhalation through both nostrils. Focus on flexing every muscle as you deepen the connection between your mind and body.

Rabbit [Sasangasana] - start in childs pose. Bring each hand back to the heels and the forehead as close to the knees as the spine will allow. Lift the hips and roll onto the top of the skull to receive an upper shoulder stretch while simultaneously activating the crown.

Fire log [Agnistambhasana] - sit upright and cross one leg over the other. Send energy up your spine towards your crown.

Fire log [Agnistambhasana]- don't forget to bring the corners of your mouth towards your ears. Smile. Your body is a gift, treat it with respect and love.

Agnistambhasana variation: supported double pigeon with block - place a block or a pillow under the knee if the hips need more space to stretch. Feel the energy rise up the spine towards your crown.

Reclined easy pose [supta sukhasana] - cross the legs and gently recline the upper body backwards onto the mat. Allow gravity to push down on the knees and activate the hips. Send that energy up the spine towards your crown.

Reclined easy pose [supta sukhasana]

Tall mountain [tadasana] - evenly distribute your weight over both feet while activating the legs and core. Feel your spine elongate as you lengthen your skull to the sky, lift through the sides of the body, and ground down through the feet.

Tree [vrksasana] - bend the knee and place the foot above or below the opposite knee. Open the hips and activate the core as your crown lifts towards the sky, lengthening the spine.

Transitions to couch pose [Paryankasana]:

> Begin on your knees similar to the preparation for camel pose. Push the hips forward with the hands and let the chest extend forward as the shoulders fall backwards.

> Reach back for each heel and continue to extend the hips and chest forwards.

Bend each elbow as the upper body slowly reclines backwards and the hips sit between the feet. Continue to look behind you as the head and neck will receive a deep stretch here.

Couch pose [Paryankasana] - reach the arms above the head and reach for the opposite elbows. Feel the energy running from the knees to the crown. You are activating your entire body in this asana. Exit this pose the same way you entered. Protect the neck by tucking the chin to the chest and use the hands to lift the hips back to a kneeling position.

# Healthy habits to support your crown chakra

Have faith and trust in the belief that the Universe works with you and everything happens for an important reason.

- Prioritize your sleep routine:
    - Keep the space around your bed free of clutter and make your bed every morning.
    - Thrift any worn out pillows or blankets and invest in a quality mattress or mattress topper.
    - Purify the air in your bedroom by frequently opening the windows to allow fresh air to circulate. Use a diffuser throughout the night or light incense to help cleanse the room before falling asleep.
    - Turn your phone on airplane mode whilst sleeping and ensure it is kept off the bed. Remove the television or any other recreational electronics out of the bedroom. Your bedroom should be a sanctuary of high frequency energy for rejuvenating the mind and body. Any distractions or technology can hinder your sleeping patterns.
    - Allow your mind and body thirty minutes to wake up before turning on any electronics or reading any texts/ emails.
- Revamp your shower routine:
    - Tie eucalyptus branches on the shower head so the leaves are in direct line with the stream of water.  The steam of the shower releases oils from the eucalyptus reducing nasal congestion, headaches and sinus infections, adding a rejuvenating element to your shower.
    - Finish every shower running cold water over your head. Acclimate your body to this practice by running hot water for 30 seconds and immediately switch to extremely cold for 30 seconds. Follow this pattern three times, finishing with cold water. Hot showers are beneficial for preventing colds, accelerating the metabolism, and tightening the skin. Cold showers reduce fatigue and headaches whilst relieving nasal congestion and relaxing the muscles. Ending your daily shower with cold water helps stimulate the brain and

promote mental clarity. By utilizing both temperatures in your wellness regime, you consistently reap the benefits.

- ⚛ Use the quality time to set positive intentions or speak any affirmations for your day.
- ⚛ Envision any fears, problems, or anxieties rinsing off your mind and body falling into the drain.

❖ Explore floatation therapy:

- ⚛ Floating is a tranquil therapeutic practice stimulating the body's natural ability to heal and regenerate through deep relaxation. It consists of floating in a tank filled with magnesium sulfate solution and heated water to match the temperature of your skin. The density of the water allows your body to float effortlessly and mental stress fades away.
- ⚛ The aim of the experience of floating is to diminish sources of physical and emotional stress by calming the adrenals. Deepen your breathwork while floating to rejuvenate your mind and strengthen your connection to your higher self. Incorporating floatation therapy into your mindfulness regimen will help improve overall well-being by reducing physical pain, ameliorate sleeping patterns, and minimizing stress.
- ⚛ Research flotation centers in your city or town and schedule a session.

❖ Experience a chromotherapy sauna session:

- ⚛ Chromotherapy is a science using vibrations of color to balance body frequencies to promote internal harmony and improve overall well-being. The full spectrum of visible light radiating from a color therapy lamp works on various energy points to support the body in the regenerative healing process.
- ⚛ When chromotherapy is integrated with an infrared sauna, the individual experiences an intense detox. The physical body begins to release toxins and impurities through sweat while simultaneously absorbing the positive energy healing from the therapeutic lights.
- ⚛ Routine sessions in a chromotherapy sauna can help calm the nervous system, reduce anxiety, alleviate insomnia, stimulate the

production of white blood cells, support healthy weight loss, and heal inflammation.

⚛ Research a center near your home and schedule a session.

✧ Meet with an experienced Kinesiologist:

⚛ Kinesiology is defined as the study of mechanics of bodily movements. It is a form of therapy that detects imbalances in the body that may develop into physical or emotional illness. The imbalances are discovered through muscle monitoring or biofeedback.

⚛ Kinesiology improves various dimensions of wellness as it deepens the relationship with the physical and emotional body. These sessions educate you about where your body specifically holds stress and explains how the physical tension relates to an emotional burden you are currently living with. The energy healing and body work of kinesiology is helpful in managing depression, reducing anxiety, confronting anger, releasing grief, strengthening joint mobility, and improving sleeping patterns.

⚛ Explore various kinesiologists in your city or town and book a session with a relatable clinician.

✧ Experience the healing power of Reiki energy:

⚛ Reiki is a holistic therapy that uses a non-invasive approach to transfer Universal energy through the practitioner's palms to the client's body. These healings are remarkably relaxing and require minimal effort from the client. The client is guided through a beginning meditation before the healing energy of reiki, channeled through the practitioner, guides them into deep meditative state.

⚛ Reiki energy breaks down blocked energy in the chakras while strengthening the body's self-healing abilities. This healing modality balances the mind, body, and spirit by reducing stress, minimizing brain fog, increasing physical energy and strengthening the body's natural circadian rhythms. One can expect to experience a stronger psychological awareness and connection between mind and body following a reiki healing.

- Look inward, not outward:

  - Start praying and build a connection with a higher dimension. Talk to your higher self — he/she is here for you. Talk to your deceased loved ones. Talk to your ancestors.
  - Ask yourself for guidance, advice, or support. The answers to your questions will come from within. Your family and friends love and support you, but they may not always have the answer or advice you are searching for. Look to yourself for any question you may have, silence the Ego, release control of the outcome, and the answers will come in beautiful ways.

## *Affirmations to open your crown chakra*

*I am divinely guided as an energetic being.*

*I am an extension of the universe and connected to a higher power. When I am in Alignment with my higher power, I bring inner peace to myself and share that nourishment with the world.*

*All is well.*

PART 4

# APPLICATION

### How to apply the strategies you've learned

# Successfully Implementing the Chakra-Energizing Habits

There is a plethora of information regarding the history, purpose, and activation of the chakra system. It may feel overwhelming, given the information may appear intimidatingly endless.

Do not allow any fear to deter you from starting. It is not as intense as it may seem, which is why an optimistic outlook is essential. It's a truly enjoyable process improving your external and internal environment to ensure you love the world around you. Your attitude and desire to create a more balanced, harmonious life will help you through the difficult days on your healing journey.

If you are indecisive about where to begin, it would be beneficial to note any section in the text that struck a nerve and inspired you to evaluate your current lifestyle. Additionally, write down your personal and professional goals. Visualize what successes and milestones you would like to reach as well as anything you wish to remove from your life. Use these goals and the highlighted chapters as guides for which area of your body you wish to heal first.

Once you have determined your current goals and the chakra you plan on energizing first, understand and implement these next six factors as you begin your activation process.

## Accept what you can and can't control

In life, there are countless things you simply cannot change. The earth will continue to orbit around the sun. The seasons will change. Your favorite sports team will lose a game. Taxes exist. The American presidential election will take place every four years. The stock market fluctuates. Your car will need an oil change every 3000 miles. People will get sick. Your loved ones will age. People will behave a certain way. The sun will set every evening. There are countless occurrences in everyday life outside of your control.

Nevertheless, you have autonomy over multiple areas in your life and control more than you think. You have control over the city or town you live in, the people you socialize with, the amount of time spent on social media and your occupation. You control the food on your plate, how many calories you consume, and the pace at which you eat. You control how often you dine out and how many drinks you enjoy during happy hour.

You control the time you wake up in the morning and the time you fall asleep at night. You are the only person in charge of your finances and how you choose to enjoy your earnings. You choose the partner you have and the circle of friends you associate with. You can choose the workout regimen you like best and how often you partake in it or train at the gym. You control the amount of television you watch, the books you read, and the social media accounts you follow.

You have free rein over the clothes you wear and how you choose to express yourself through accessories, body art, and hairstyles. You control the decor of your home, the car you drive and how you balance your work and life responsibilities. You control your daily habits, your reactions to all situations, and your emotions. Lastly, and most importantly, you control your thoughts and how you maintain your physical and emotional body.

Accept the things you cannot change and place your energy on things you can. Understanding where you have autonomy in your life positively directs your energy. Showing up and caring for your physical and mental health foremost, will help you become a stronger partner, friend, colleague, and member of society. When you cultivate and protect your own energy you will be able to show up for your personal and professional responsibilities with a more confident and poised attitude.

Whichever career or life path you choose, activating the energy of your chakras strengthens your self-assurance in that path. In regard to change on a micro level, you may be able to use your power to positively influence someone's behaviors, thoughts, or beliefs. However, it is important to accept others and their lifestyle choices for what they are. This respect will be returned to you.

When instigating change on a macro level, you will become a more powerful vessel of change when you are fiercely confident and secure in your words and actions. This confidence is derived from strengthening your solar plexus and throat chakras. The energy centers embedded in your body are intended to help you positively advance in life. Prioritize the care of your chakras and use this powerful energy for good.

You have 100% responsibility for everything that happens in your life. Take accountability for the things you control. You control your body and how you maintain it. Do not allow external factors to hinder your physical and emotional well-being.

It does not matter what the weather is like, how the stock market is performing, who is the elected president, or what your neighbors are doing. You control yourself and your lifestyle choices. Prioritize your mental, physical and emotional health. You are the only person capable of activating your own chakras and strengthening the energy that exists in your body. No one can do this work for you.

## Acknowledge and improve your self-talk

Thoughts and words carry their own vibrational frequencies. The language you speak and surround yourself with directly impacts the vibrational frequencies of your chakras. The physical and emotional body directly responds to internal dialogue and the language of the environment, lowering its vibration if surrounded by negative or abusive language, while rising when absorbing loving, affirmative words.

The way you speak to yourself and how you allow others to speak to you is exceptionally important when healing your physical and emotional body. Your physical body responds more positively when it hears a high frequency thought compared to a lower, more negative thought. Bring awareness to your everyday mental chatter and assess how you typically speak to and about yourself. It is important to use high vibrational language as you are trying to increase the frequency of your body and mind.

The success of activating your chakras is dependent on your inner dialogue and the way you view yourself. Acknowledge the different frequencies of the following statements and how the body and mind respond. Use these as inspiration for raising the vibrational frequency of your language and reframing your thought patterns.

## Subtle ways to improve your self-talk

**Low frequency thought:** I have to exercise today. I hate my body and I have to lose weight.
**High frequency thought:** I am really looking forward to moving my body today. My body and mind respond well to weight training and deep yoga stretching.

**Low frequency thought:** I am so frumpy and sluggish. I have no energy and I feel gross.
**High frequency thought:** There are some days I feel bright and confident but today is not one of them. I am still beautiful even when I'm tired.

**Low frequency thought:** I cannot believe I have hustled all day and still did not finish my to-do list. Now tomorrow is going to be extra hectic.
**High frequency thought:** I am so proud of myself for making my to-do list smaller. I will do my best to make it even smaller tomorrow.

**Low frequency thought:** I am so disappointed in myself. I didn't receive the promotion I have been striving all year for.
**High frequency thought:** There must be a better opportunity coming my way. I am confident and have faith that the universe will present me with something that aligns with me more.

**Low frequency thought:** My partner had the audacity to leave me and now I am single and lonely. How am I expected to date and fall in love again at this age?
**High frequency thought:** Every person who enters my life teaches me an important lesson and they can leave at any time. It is my responsibility to energetically fill my own cup and have no attachments to others. The relationship I have with myself is the most important one I have.

**Low frequency thought:** I studied for this exam for weeks and didn't receive an A. I am not a B+ student, I am much smarter than that.

**High frequency thought:** I intensely prepared for this exam and am proud of myself for this grade. I am very intelligent and have a great study ethic — my grades will continue to improve throughout the year.

**Low frequency thought:** I don't understand why I am still single after all these years. I hold such great qualities and would be an amazing partner.

**High frequency thought:** I will be an amazing partner when I am ready to welcome love into my life. I am whole by myself and will complement the right person perfectly.

**Low frequency thought:** I give more to others than they give to me. People are constantly draining me.

**High frequency thought:** Some people cannot hold space for me like I can for them. I know my energy will always be returned and am happy to help those around me.

Observe the different frequencies and feelings these statements possess. The Ego wants to find and dwell on the negative, but it is crucial to be stronger than the Ego. Train your mind to find a positive element in every situation.

It can often be difficult to find the positives in negative circumstances, but it is important when helping your body physically and emotionally evolve. Fight the urge to think negatively and make it a habit to find gratitude and positivity in everything. This minor perspective change, when implemented frequently, will have a monumental impact on your overall attitude and energy. The mental shift will be inevitable.

Your strength and power derive from your inner dialogue. The words you speak to yourself influence your belief system. Belief changes biology and plays a significant role when starting to heal your body and mind. If you truly believe you can cognitively or physically accomplish a specific goal, grant yourself the opportunity to reach it.

You must be kind and gentle with yourself. The activation of the chakras will not be an enjoyable or successful process if you are mean and hateful to yourself. Your body does not respond positively to hate. It is crucial to show your physical and emotional body copious amounts of love during this process. Setting and achieving high standards for yourself does not require aggressive, judgmental or cruel self-talk. You will blossom when you speak loving and kind words to yourself, despite how chaotic your day has been.

## Create an environment for success

A plant's environment will either promote its prosperity or destroy its growth process. Plants require proper soil, water, sunlight, and nutrients to help them develop. If they do not receive these essential elements on a regular basis, they will not grow to their greatest ability. Consistency is vital. Consequently, plants need attention and time to grow. The perfect environment for plant growth includes routine care, patience, and love.

The same is required for personal development. You need to provide yourself with the ideal environment to support your physical, mental and spiritual growth. Chakra activation requires consistent effort over a length of time — you'll truly flourish when your home, work environment, and mental space are congruent.

It is critical to objectively evaluate the physical and mental environment you currently live in. Use these questions to guide your evaluation:

- Is your home overwhelmed with clutter and unused items?
- How organized is your fridge?
- Is your pantry filled with healthy food items to prepare convenient healthy snacks and meals, or is it filled with junk food?
- Do you sleep on old bedding with flat pillows?
- Is your wardrobe full of old clothes that do not complement your style anymore?
- How well do you maintain your car?
- Does your gym bag contain three dirty outfits, your missing belt, and all your unwashed blender bottles?
- When was the last time your work desk was organized and cleaned?
- Is your email flooded with promotions and insignificant junk? Are you meticulous about your finances?
- Do you know when your credit bill is due?
- Is the appropriate paperwork organized and prepared to pay your income taxes by their due date?
- Have you called your best friend recently?
- Did you remember your partner's birthday is next week?

Ensuring your mind and personal sanctuaries are organized, free of clutter, and clean will positively influence the progression of chakra activation. When your body and mind are provided with healthy environments that promote growth and well-being, you will begin to heal and feel better with time.

It is crucial to consistently maintain your physical environment as it directly impacts your mental health. However, this process does not happen overnight or even after a month. It takes time and commitment. Though, when an individual takes pride in their environments and habitually performs these chakra cleansing techniques, they will noticeably reap the benefits as time progresses.

## Drink more H20

Double the amount of water you drink daily.

Drinking clean water is the first step to revitalizing your physical and spiritual body.

This step does not need to be overly strenuous. Try adding fresh lemon, oranges, cucumber, apples or mint to your drinking water. This simple step adds extra beneficial nutrients, flavor, and excitement.

Give your cells the opportunity to rejuvenate from this straightforward, yet necessary step. As a result, your emotions will begin to even out and brain fog will dissipate.

Aim for three to four liters daily.

## Be consistent in your actions

The mindfulness habits associated with chakra activation are not strenuous and can be easily integrated into the busiest lifestyle. Nonetheless, the consistency of these habits will contribute to the success of your chakra activation. These minor lifestyle improvements will have a lasting impact on your overall well-being when routinely incorporated into your daily life.

The trick to consistency is making these habits as simple and convenient as possible. The less complicated these habits are, the easier they will be to consistently integrate into your busy days.

## Simple ways to sneak habits into your daily life

- ❁ Keep your crystals by your bedside table and hold them before drifting asleep.
- ❁ Leave a vial of your favorite essential oils in the shower so you can inhale the scent or add a few drops to your body soap.
- ❁ Purchase frozen smoothie ingredients in bulk to keep in the freezer for a convenient addition to your breakfast.
- ❁ Save your daily, weekly, or monthly affirmation as a background on your phone so it is consistently seen throughout the day.
- ❁ Keep a small bottle of essential oil infused spray in your purse or car for a quick aura cleanse.
- ❁ Open your yoga mat and keep it in the space where you enjoy spending the most time and will always see it. Step on your mat and practice a few asanas prior to relaxing.
- ❁ Use a journal to help stay organized on your daily tasks, list your intention and affirmations, and remember any inspiration or ideas that come to you. Keep this journal where you will see it and write in it often. Personalize it and treat it with respect.
- ❁ Invest in a water filter. Establish a daily intake goal and mark that goal on the filter. Store it where you will constantly be reminded to drink water.

These chakra-activating habits do not need to be daunting or strenuous. It is important to keep them as manageable and simple as possible. The simplicity of these habits will make it easy to consistently incorporate mindfulness into your daily life. Implementing mindfulness habits over a prolonged period of time will have the most profound impact on your overall well-being and activation of the chakras.

## Simply begin and enjoy the journey

Self-care should not wait until Sunday. Adding a small mindfulness practice everyday will result in greater success overtime. Begin with any practice that resonates with you at this moment. Implement it into your daily routine and celebrate the improvement that transpires over several weeks.

Then, gradually add a second and third mindfulness practice into your routine. Enjoy the process of trying new habits and observing how the body and mind adapts to the minor, yet impactful changes.

Focus on the journey, not the destination. Being fixated on the outcome removes the excitement out of personal development, which is a truly enjoyable process. Acknowledge the breakthroughs throughout your efforts and be proud of them. These breakthroughs could be perceived as strengthening how you communicate with your partner, increasing the nutrients in your diet, improving your sleep cycles, or feeling less anxious and more confident in yourself.

Any improvement to your life making you feel mentally and physically better is a milestone on your journey. Awareness and appreciation of the minor changes to your lifestyle is incredibly important as they contribute to your soul's evolution.

The goal is to create a longevity of inner peace for yourself — something that isn't a quick fix. Chakra activation continuously occurs throughout our human life and can be an amazing experience if you are aware of it. Devotion, consistency, and gratitude are essential in activating the chakras, raising your vibration, spiritually evolving, and reaching enlightenment.

# Conclusion

The chakras are centers of invisible energy in the human body keeping you lively, vibrant, and balanced every day. Every human being currently lives with their own chakra system, and the innate ability to activate it.

Chakras are not contingent on age, gender, socioeconomic status, or cultural background. We all have them. This similarity connects us to one another on a mental, physical, and spiritual level. Regardless of your conscious awareness of chakras, they still exist in your body and directly impact your mental and physical wellbeing.

It is extremely profound that information about the ancient chakra system is accessible for all. We have utilized chakra-activating practices for thousands of years and continuously share the effectiveness of them to support the evolution of humanity. As one individual reaps the benefits of these practices and achieves inner peace, they will begin to attract an abundance of love, health, and wealth into their life. This prosperity will positively impact others around them.

Similarly, as one embodies the benefits of spiritual wellness, they will demonstrate to others how to activate the power within their own bodies to create a peaceful, abundant life. The positive outcomes gained from activating the chakras are achievable for all who consciously seek them.

The chakras vibrate on the same frequency as the body and mind. If you wish to heal, energize, and raise the frequencies of each chakra, you must raise the overall vibration of your body. Become aware of your thoughts, as everything you feel, think, and speak will become reality. Make time for the things you are passionate about. Express gratitude daily, speak kindly to yourself, eat mindfully, drink plenty of water, meditate frequently, move your body every day, and practice acts of kindness for yourself and others. These positive habits will help improve the wellbeing of your mental and physical body and start to activate your chakras.

Your chakras work for you, but they need to be energized to function efficiently. When your body receives adequate exercise, nutritious food, proper sleep and regular meditation, your chakras will actively move stagnant energy in your body. This energetic shift will positively impact any physical pain or emotional ailment you may experience. As emotional and physical burdens dissipate, your body will reach a homeostasis contributing to the improvement of your overall life.

This spiritual shift requires intention, practice, and time. Having acknowledged this, the shift is remarkably delightful and dependent on one's perspective and attitude towards it. If feelings of confusion or skepticism surface while exploring these practices, take a deep breath and slowly exhale.

It is pivotal to remember that our physical bodies evolved from earth, and are not machines. Take your journey at a pace that's compatible with your current lifestyle. Do not overwhelm your mind and body by immediately implementing numerous practices, which results in burnout weeks later. Begin with any practice that resonates at this exact moment.

Start small, and enjoy the process.

One minute of meditation for 60 days is more effective than 60 minutes of meditation for one day. Trying a daily yoga pose for three months is more effective, for body, mind and spirit, than practicing 21 postures over the length of three days. This process consists of minor actions to take over a prolonged period of time with a significant amount of patience — the desired outcome for the activation of the chakras is to create an enjoyable, sustainable lifestyle.

Achieving balanced wellness is not a sprint - it's a lifelong journey. There is no quick fix. Start small, but start today. Be gentle with your words and disciplined in your actions. Your future self will thank you as you begin to feel balanced while managing all the chaos life brings.

# Acknowledgments

Writing a book is harder than I originally thought and more rewarding than I could have ever imagined. I enjoyed every single moment working on this guide as it truly brought me so much joy and excitement. It took an immense amount of work and it would not exist without the inevitable contributions of a number of incredibly talented, supportive, and intelligent people.

Thank you to my brilliant editor and fellow nomad, Angus Kennelly. I am eternally grateful for you and your dedication to this project. Simply put, you are incredible, and this book is more powerful because of you.

Thank you to my beautiful photographer, Polina Levina. We have endured Australian summer storms, insane ocean currents, chilly sunsets and sweltering heat together just to get the perfect shots. Your work is amazing. Thank you for continuing to stay optimistic during every photo shoot even as you were laying in dirt, getting soaked by the ocean, standing in random flower patches and embracing all uncertainties that come with the Australian seasons.

Thank you to the amazing Alex Fullerton, the woman behind Author Support Services, for your guidance and expertise. You are an inspiration and I have learned countless valuable lessons from you. I look forward to working with you on many future projects.

Thank you to my illustrator, Melanie Howarth. Okay, that felt weird calling you my illustrator. Girl, you're like family. Thank you for bringing my stick figure vision to life and optimistically enduring the mental stress of this project. The cover art is absolutely incredible, and this book would not be the same without your artwork and unconditional support. Sister, what a journey this year has been. I'd like to open that can of worms right now and I could actually write another book just talking about our friendship. Y'all know I love a nice, detailed story, but we'll save that one for another time.

Sometimes this life feels like a movie, or a musical, if you will. It could not go on without the stage crew and all the help behind the scenes. Simply put, I have an amazing foundation of family and friends (who have become like family) that wholeheartedly believe in me and continuously offer their support. These people have helped me become the woman, teacher, and writer I am today.

To my mentors, Lyza, Shauna, and Vivian, thank you for your lessons, compassion, guidance, and humor. You make the world a brighter place and I am privileged to know you.

To my Aussie yoga and reiki students, I cannot fully express my appreciation for y'all in a short paragraph. Scott, Fiorella, Lama, Ben, Bianca, Brenton, Andrew S., Erin, Justin, Andrew H., and Milan: It has been an absolute pleasure serving you on your mindfulness journeys. Your dedication to your physical and mental health and unwavering trust in me has truly grounded me in Brisbane during this unprecedented moment in time. You guys are an inspiration and encourage me to become a stronger teacher every single day. Thank you for welcoming me into your homes and offices each week and embodying the philosophy of yoga with an open mind. I feel honored to watch your yoga practices expand as you grow into even stronger versions of yourselves.

I would like to thank my New England friends who graciously loaned me their chakras when I transitioned from mental health counseling to energy healing. I received an abundance of support from a variety of friend groups, which encouraged me to leave my city, travel across the world, start a business, and write a book.

To the friends I flipped tables with at the Red Stripe, dug through trash looking for lost credit cards on the fourth of July at the Atlantic, shucked oysters at 19Raw with, partied at 688 River, and completed my yoga teacher training with: thank you for your loving support of my journey and trusting me with your bodies when as I started practicing reiki healing.  I will never forget the days when I started doing healings at 107 John street and on the beaches on Martha's Vineyard. Those days and the people who helped me gain confidence in this field are insanely important to me. Thank you. I love y'all more than you know.

To my amazing family, Iaccarinos rule! I am so blessed to be a part of the best team around. Through my family, I have learned the most important lessons this life can offer: the value of unconditional love, the virtue of patience, the selflessness of forgiveness, and above all else, "laughter is the best medicine".

Dottie, Tony, Andrew, Lindsay, Phil, Greg, and Hogan — you are all incredibly unique and inspire me to become the best version of myself every day. To our guardian angel, John Francis McKiernan, thank you for watching over our clan and guiding us along our paths. I feel as if there are dimes being thrown at my freckled face every week, and these signs keep us going. If you know, you know.

Goodness, I almost forgot to mention my favorite musicians. That would have been a legitimate crime. I really need to emphasize how impactful these artists and their music are. I literally listened to San Holo's "Stay Vibrant" album for, kid you not, 95 days straight. The entire album was at the top of my 2020 Spotify playlist and all my friends asked, "Girl, you good?" I was so good. This album inspired me so much. In addition to San Holo, it's crucial I acknowledge Hazlett, Sol Rising, Noah Kahan, Ziggy Alberts and Xavier Rudd. I passionately believe music keeps this world spinning on its axis. Please keep writing and producing your music, we need it and deeply appreciate it.

Lastly, and truthfully the most important, I need to thank God and the Divine Feminine. Without God's love and unwavering support, I would not have been able to complete this piece. All things are possible with faith in Him.

# About the Author

Sarah Iaccarino brings a spirited personality and effervescent attitude to the healing world. Combining her skills as a mental health counselor, yoga teacher, and Reiki healer, she is an advocate for individuals of all socioeconomic backgrounds accessing quality mental health care and spiritual guidance. Sarah is dedicated to integrating the healing qualities of Eastern medicine with the Westernized world.

Sarah travels around the world teaching the effectiveness of these arcane therapeutic modalities in group workshops and individual sessions. She works with a diverse clientele and focuses on the utilization of the chakra system and various mindfulness techniques to attract prosperous health and abundance for themselves.

Explore www.healwithaligntherapies.com for upcoming workshops and additional resources.

# Bibliography

1. *CREATING A HEALTHIER LIFE: A STEP-BY-STEP GUIDE TO WELLNESS.* Substance Abuse and Mental Health Services Association, 2016.

2. Cooper, N.J., and Schneider, Adalbert. *A Brief History of the Chakras in Human Body.* Pennsylvania State University, 2019.

3. Bailey, James. "Discover the Ida and Pingala Nadis." Yoga Journal, 5 April 2007, www.yogajournal.com/yoga-101/balancing-act-2.

4. "Chakra Basics." International Association of Reiki Professionals, iarp. org/chakra-basics.

5. Palermo, Elizabeth. "Crystal Healing: Stone-Cold Facts About Gemstone Treatments." Live Science, 23 June 2017, www.livescience.com/40347-crystal-healing.html.

6. Shine, Teketa. "A Beginner's Guide to Clearing, Cleansing, and Charging Crystals." HEALTHLINE Media, 19 September 2018, www.healthline.com/health/pain-relief/surprising-natural-pain-killers.

7. Azeemi, Samina T Yousuf, and S Mohsin Raza. "A Critical Analysis of Chromotherapy and Its Scientific Evolution". Evidence-based complementary and alternative medicine, 2005.

8. Segal, Inna. The Secret Language of Your Body: The Essential Guide to Healing. Beyond Words Publishing, 2010.

9. "Aromatherapy History." Aromatherapy.com, 2018, www.aromatherapy.com/history.

10. Cottrell, John. "Yoga Essentials." Trickle, trickle.app/drip/14130-the-sun-salutation-is-the-most-popular-flow-for-beginners/.

11. Carrico, Mara. "Get to Know the Eight Limbs of Yoga". Yoga Journal, 10 July 2017, www.yogajournal.com/practice/the-eight-limbs.

12. "What are Brainwaves?" Symphonic Mind, www.brainworksneurotherapy.com/what-are-brainwaves.

13. Cooper, Belle. "What Happens to the Brain When You Meditate." LifeHacker, 26 August 2013, www.lifehacker.com/what-happens-to-the-brain-when-you-meditate-and-how-it-1202533314.

14. " Nose Breathing vs. Mouth Breathing - Which is Better?." Breathing.com, www.breathing.com/pages/nose-breathing.

15. Giovanni. "Trataka Meditation: Still Eyes, Still Mind." Live & Dare, 2017, www.liveanddare.com/trataka/#disqus_thread.

16. Yrizarry, Shannon. "7 Teas to Balance Your Chakras". DailyLife.com, 20 September 2019, www.dailylife.com/article/7-teas-to-balance-your-chakras.

17. "Food for your chakras". Times of India, 14 July 2013, www.timesofindia. indiatimes.com/life-style/health-fitness/diet/Food-for-your-chakras/articleshow/19661214.cms.

18. "Chakra Guide." Best Crystals, www.bestcrystals.com/pages/chakra-guide.

19. "Law of Vibration." Laws of the Universe, https://lawsoftheuniverse.weebly.com/law-of-vibration.html

20. "Nasa Confirms: Sun Gazing Has Healing Properties" What is Sungazing, https://www.wellnessoneofredding.com/blog/60878-nasa-confirms-sun-gazing-has-healing-properties